The NarrowRoad™

A Guide to Legacy Wealth

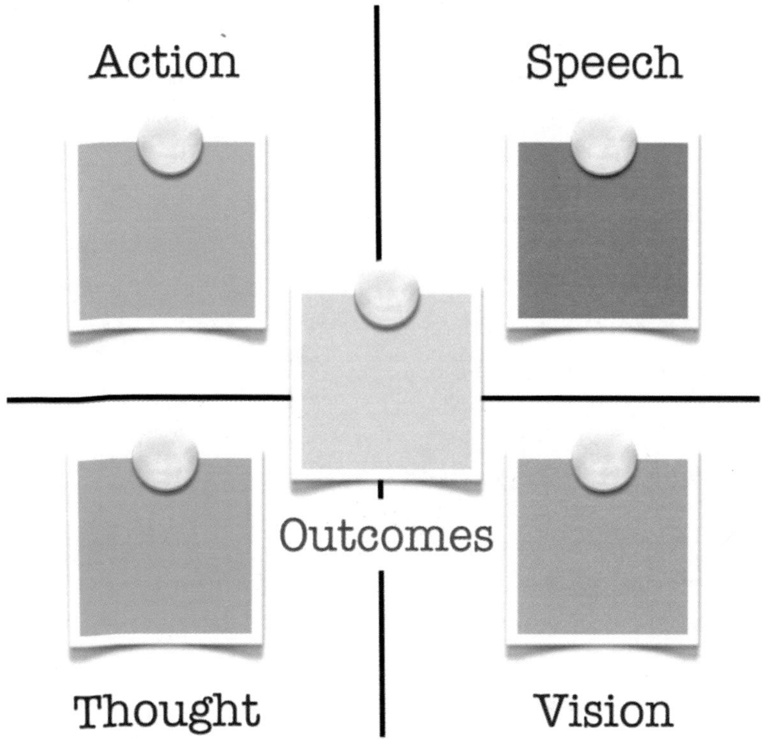

By Pamela Jolly

The NarrowRoad™

Books may be ordered by contacting

Torchlight Publishing

3225 McLeod Drive, Suite 100

Las Vegas, NV 89121

202-656-5593

Visit mynarrowroadbook.com.

ISBN: 978-0-9966141-7-7

Printed in the United States of America.

This Book is Dedicated to the Torch Bearers of My Legacy

Great-Great Grandparents

Joseph Jolly & Lillie Brown Jolly

James Horne & Jane Horne

William Harrington & Ella Jane Ratliff

Great Grandparents

Fred Watkins & Ethel Pearl DeBerry Watkins

Floyd R. Morgan & Gertrude Hutton Morgan

Melvin Jolly & Lillian Ruffin Jolly

John Horne & Roxanne Horne

Grandparents

Alphonso Jolly Sr. & Mildred Lorraine Morgan Jolly

Bennie Lee Horne Sr. & Bessie Pearl Watkins Horne

Parents

Vincent Creswell Jolly Sr. & Sylvia Mae Horne Jolly

My Dear Sibling

Vincent Creswell Jacob Jolly Jr.

Contents

A Note to the Reader

Matthew 7:13-14 is the scripture that supports the NarrowRoad™ it is from the final teachings of Jesus Christ in the Sermon on the Mount. The Sermon contains the central tenets of Christian discipleship. This scripture puts the NarrowRoad™ in perspective when you replace the word "gate" with "road." Merriam-Webster has seven definitions of the term "narrow", six of which have a negative connotation. The most fitting definition at the crux of Dr. Pamela Jolly's life passion of legacy wealth is:

Narrow: careful, thorough, or minute, as a scrutiny, search, or inquiry. Road: a way or course

The NarrowRoad™ is just that...a carefully laid out process that is unique to each reader while connecting to their defined promised land, legacy wealth, community, and culture.

What's in it for you (the reader)? I can only answer that by telling you what was in it for me. I have seen The NarrowRoadTM since it's conception in 2004. Pamela's passion about legacy wealth creation was so far above my head and my "check-to-check" situation that I thought wealth was a foreign unattainable object. I heard her define capital in a various forms, but could only "see" the green paper side of capital. I realized that I was sitting on a gold mine of both intellectual capital and social capital.

It took me 9 years to FINALLY see the light and turn that capital into wealth. Going through The NarrowRoad Identity, I am a "Doer" in the first quadrant. That means I have to "do it, to get it." I am a hands-on person. In February 2013, I became an entrepreneur. I started my consulting firm based on my intellectual capital and social capital, but more importantly because I had a guide to help me through my process. This guide is so much more than a "how-to" approach, it's an approach that plays to your strengths and weaknesses; not only in your professional life, but in your personal life as well.

I have known Pamela since high school. I drove down to Hampton University (my first time driving on the highway) to watch her receive her Bachelor's. I drove to University of Pennsylvania's Wharton School of Business with a BBQ Chicken Pizza to help her through one of her stressful nights while earning her MBA. I was there when she returned from New Orleans after her rebuilding efforts post-Katrina. I was there when she left for Boston's Theological Seminary on the same path that Dr. Martin Luther King, Jr. prodded to receive her doctorate. Today, I continue to travel to as many speaking engagements I can make to see her discuss legacy wealth. What I enjoy the most of the many years spent with Pamela, is to see God's answers revealed for prayers we prayed years ago and watching others in the room and seeing their light bulb moment.

My definition of wealth may not see me on the cover of Forbes, but I know that what I have created will leave a legacy for my child and community thanks to Dr. Pamela C.V. Jolly, my closest friend, and The NarrowRoad™. — **Keisha L'Rae Chandler**

He that is in the shadow of wisdom is in the shadow of money, for wisdom is the cause why riches come.

— Ecclesiastes 7:12

Glossary of Terms

During my research I asked thousands of people to define seven key words. The process revealed that while we say the same words, we often do not mean the same things, and as a result, a lot gets lost in translation when we talk about wealth, legacy and money. To address this I chose to begin this book with a glossary of terms. Along the NarrowRoad you will come to own these definitions in your pursuit of legacy wealth.

Acumen—the ability to make shrewd and strategic decisions

Capital—wealth in the form of money or other assets owned by a person or organization.

Capital, cultural—your perspective based on the lived experiences of you, your family, and your community. Cultural capital is unique to you and your legacy; it is the lens through which you can see what others cannot initially see.

Capital, human—knowledge, skills, experiences, intuition, and attitudes used to earn income in the workforce

Capital, intellectual— applied knowledge that is of value, useful for establishing partnerships to grow

Capital, social—who you know, how you connect, and the way in which you exchange value

Capital, spiritual—what you believe, who you believe, why you believe, and how you affirm your faith in what you believe

Capital exchanges—there are four "capital exchanges" along the NarrowRoad. Capital exchanges are the ways in which you exchange the five resources you have in your portfolio of talents.

Exchange 1: Sympathetic Capital—an exchange where you jump all in into another persons current situation to assist others

Exchange 2: Empathetic Capital—an exchange where you partially enter into another persons current situation to assist others

Exchange 3: Apathetic Capital—an exchange where you avoid situations that require you to assist others not on par with your standard of living

Exchange 4: Compassionate Capital—an exchange where you invite others to consider the solution you have taken to address an issue or situation they are currently facing.

Entrepreneur—a person who organizes and operates a business or businesses, taking on greater than normal financial risks in order to do so.

Financial equity—the value of an ownership interest in property, including shareholders' equity in a business. Equity or shareholders′ equity is part of the total capital of a business.

Financial literacy—the ability to use knowledge and skills to manage one's financial resources effectively for lifetime financial security

Financial plan—a report that identifies a person's financial goals, needs, and expected future earning, saving, investing, insurance, and debt management activities; it typically includes a statement of net worth (equity) and an ongoing thinking process to develop an orderly program or blueprint for handling all aspects of one's money, including spending, credit, saving, and investing.

Intrapreneurship—the act of behaving like an entrepreneur while working within a large organization

Legacy—a narrative that did not begin with you and will not end with you unless you remain "stuck" in your financial wilderness story

Legacy wealth—the convergence of one's faith in his or her future and the ongoing financial stewardship of past and present resources. Legacy wealth is used to successfully navigate out of the financial wilderness and onto a path toward promise.

Margin of safety—a metric used to gain a better understanding of the impact of change or loss of income to your current financial situation.

NRID—your NarrowRoad ID, a code that once applied to your life reveals your "system of success" path toward legacy wealth.

NREQ—the NarrowRoad equation. A string of variables that when pursued in sequence results in the possession of a desired outcome

Personal finance—the principles and methods individuals use to acquire and manage income and assets

Quantum Leap — a carefully executed path beyond the financial wilderness using your NRID in the four terrains (rocky, thorny, fertile, landmines)

Value system—a set of criteria, standards, or principles that guide an individual or group's behavior and provides a sense of direction to life

Values, cultural—prevailing beliefs and value systems of a given society passed on through social conditioning/enculturation

Values, individual—an individual's beliefs about what is important, desirable, and worthwhile, which often influence decisions

Vision, financial—a description of how an individual defines future financial success, and what he or she wants to accomplish; provides direction for decision and actions that invent the preferred future: What will the future look like if financial strategies are successfully implemented and one's full potential is achieved?

Wealth building—increasing the total value of what one owns; one's tangible assets using strategies to increase savings and personal asset accumulation, thereby promoting individual/family economic well-being and financial security

Wealth creator—a person on the NarrowRoad who is committed to creating, building, growing, and expanding legacy wealth for themselves and generations to come

Author's Note

Along The NarrowRoad, the Ultimate Desired Outcome Is Legacy Wealth

Throughout my journey, I found that everyone in some way wants to live a good, fulfilling life and pass that accomplishment onto the next generation. Yes, some of us want the next generation to learn the importance of hard work and the necessary role hard work plays in earning a life filled with creature comforts, but in addition to all of that, I have found that we also want each generation to fulfill a promise that may not have been possible in the world we inherited.

While it is sometimes hard to see how best to pass the torch to the rising generation while we are living, we all in some way want the wheel of life to move forward. In our own unique ways we sometimes secretly desire to see how our dreams and aspirations will be carried forward, and contribute to the push required to keep the legacy momentum going.

This shared desired outcome to me is legacy wealth, a cross generational narrative of progress that did not begin with us and will not end with us as long as we keep the dialog alive, relevant, and flexible to the inherent promise of the shared belief that things will get better generation after generation. The subject of the multigenerational dialog is the wealth part, wealth is I have come to intimately understand is a group process. Wealth, once self-defined, becomes the journey of how navigate your life business. This navigation is a series of twists and turns along a road that narrows with your financial decisions, decisions that build, grow, and expand over time with work, savings, and investments.

The saving and the investments aspect of each and every one of our journeys, are governed by decisions that are not just financial, they also contain tangible and intangible aspects of wealth. Intangible aspects such as knowledge, culture, relationships, and time spent remembering the purpose of our lives. These are the flames that ignite very early in our lives that when nurtured become the torch we pass on for generations.

I am convinced after talking with thousands of us that each and every one of us is here in this time and space for a unique reason. The reason did not begin with nine months in a womb and a series of pushes. It began long before that. Our ultimate desired outcome is to create a legacy for ourselves—to find a way that links the narrative of the past to our present life narrative, with the hopes that our successes and failures will create pathways that build, grow, and expand the light onto our uncharted pathways in our chosen territories. Which will make the road brighter for those in the future.

Are you the first to have pursued a road that no one in your family has navigated? Our purpose in this world is to live a life that produces fun and fruit that becomes resources for the next generation to take it even further. The road is eternal, our journey along it is a pursuit of wealth, happiness and promise however we choose to define it. Belief in our ability to connect the dots within our lifetime is how legacy and wealth meet one another along the NarrowRoad. Uncovering the fullness of who you are and where you come from to chart a path to reap the harvests uniquely available to you as a part of your inheritance is the Promise.

For every generation there is a tool that assists our collective pursuit of purpose. Ranging from Steven Covey's 7 Habits of Highly Effective People to the Carl Jung-inspired Myers-Briggs Personality Test to astrology, numerology, and religion. The longest reigning tool for identifying and pursuing one's life purpose is the basic instruction found in the bible. There are leaders whose purpose in life is to build an organized way to make sense of the world so that others can navigate with confidence and clarity their way forward. I am one of those people. The NarrowRoad is one of those tools, and we are in a time where anchoring our lives to a common yet individual outcome is needed to push the wheel of life forward to regain some of the momentum we have lost in our pursuit of happiness. More and more of us are losing sight of our way to arrive at the happiness we want with the life we have inherited. It's time to reconnect the dots of our lives to navigate a way to back to legacy wealth, however we define it.

So how do you define legacy wealth? Along the NarrowRoad this will be your desired outcome. A desired outcome is an anchor to the strategy of your life. In the Bible, it is called the Promised Land. In America, it is called the American Dream. In the world, it is the pursuit of happiness. A desired outcome remains constant until you attain it. Along the NarrowRoad your desired outcome is the guiding light at the end of your road. Your desired outcome helps you measure the progress of the legacy and the wealth you are building, growing, expanding each and every day you choose to move closer in your life purpose. Achieving a desired outcome is taking possession of an inherited promise; it is the harvest of a seed that took lifetimes to create.

I wish you extreme success in the pursuit of your desired outcomes and offer you the NarrowRoad as a tool to guide your way.

Welcome

What matters less is what's on the page but what's in your head as you read it.

—Youngme Moon

The NarrowRoad is the byproduct of my search for purpose. I sought a way to combine my love of God, business, and people. My search revealed that when it comes to our relationships with money and exchanges of things of value, we are more alike than different. The difference I have found is based on our unique legacy perspectives. Our perspectives have been molded and shaped by the people who came before us, the unique experiences we have been faced with, and the cultural obstacles we have faced along our life journey.

I have spent time exploring these differences in perspectives which appeared to me as glimpses of light in dark places such as chaos, confusion, and doubt. These "glimpses" which I refer to as our "legacy perspectives" are what gave me the eyes to see beyond the financial wilderness we all find ourselves in to the faith filled promises that remain hidden within you and me. On the following pages resides a glimpse of my unique perspective of the hidden treasure that resides in all of us.

The Jolly-Journey Overview

On the journey to discover my life's purpose, three things became clear.

1. Wealth is created every day in America by businesses and their owners who know simple principles.
2. For too many "regular people," legacy is something you talk about in small groups and at funerals, while for the wealthy, it is something you studied, owned, focused on, and kept passing forward.
3. Faith is the one thing that either unifies or is in some way leveraged by everybody when finances are tight and legacies have been forgotten.

When attempting to pursue wealth, there are many concepts that must be understood. This can seem overwhelming. My advice is to follow the wise suggestion of those who came before you: "Approach each text as if it were a new acquaintance."

Skim it.

Take in the surface details to develop a sense of what is beneath the cover.

Ask what kind of companion you want to make of it.

Journey as you see fit.

- A text of wisdom can enlighten you along your journey.
- A text of knowledge can guide you to greater understanding.
- A text of key steps can direct your need for results.
- A text of messages can assist you in overcoming your fears.

The NarrowRoad described in this book strives to be all these things. The choice of relationship is up to you.

After listening to thousands of people unknowingly share the same fears and frustrations about their relationship with money, I created this book as a "guide for the perplexed," this book is for those uncertain about how to make the best choices with all the options and talents they have been given. As you read this book, you will begin your journey down the NarrowRoad. This is significant because a narrow road to wealth has never been available like this before. A narrow road is one that few find and even fewer take, a wealth guide that follows the principles of the narrow road reveal the path toward wealth unique to you.

Your path to a deeper relationship with legacy and wealth, begins here. Only you can define wealth for you and your family. Everyone's definition will be a little different. It is my goal that you will enjoy wealth your way. I am grateful you have chosen to begin your NarrowRoad journey. Enjoy.

About My "Jolly-Journey"

I am proud to be a member of the Jolly family legacy. People will often say upon meeting me and hearing me speak that I am appropriately named. Jolly literally means to encourage someone in a lively and friendly way, journey, literally means a process of personal change and development. For the past ten years the first thing friends and family would ask me is "where in the world are you now?" I began to remark that I am "somewhere along the Jolly-journey." The response stuck and with the discovery of the NarrowRoad I began to see that I was truly on a Jolly-journey-journey, a journey where my legacy was leading me to what I was designed to do. Because I desire to journey with others along the NarrowRoad to legacy wealth—let me tell you a bit about my Jolly-journey.

With limited clarity of how, I set out to make my life matter in 2004. I had been raised in a home where faith, finance, legacy, wealth, and respect for generational wisdom were important. Finding my purpose, my way to contribute to the legacy became my main focus early in life. My father, a computer engineer, and mother, an oncology nurse, raised me in a middle-class home with rules and structure that I abided by and grew to appreciate. Once the choice was made to pursue a life of purpose, the steps of my life formed a NarrowRoad that placed me in dark, unfamiliar places, trying to catch a glimpse of light. The first glimpse of light was a question: Where do I go from here? It was 2004, and I had left my job. It had been my fourth job since graduating from The Wharton School of Business. I felt like the square peg in the round hole I had been called all my life. What I learned at Wharton is that square pegs are outliers and outliers in statistics are observation points that are distant from other observations, but regardless of their distance, they in some way are important just the same.

I discovered after ten years on the Jolly-journey that the definition of legacy wealth is unique to you and can be translated through your NarrowRoad identity (NRID). Through the NarrowRoad method you will discover that wealth resides within you, which when understood leads to the creation of a more personal definition of wealth and a roadmap to pursue it. Consider the roadmap an invitation to chart a path toward the wealth you desire to create.

In the beginning of this journey I remember asking myself, 'Is it realistic to expect a melting pot of people with different types of relationships with money and different levels of belief in what role money plays in society to all define wealth the same way?' I didn't and still don't think so. The idea of creating a pathway for individuals to define wealth their way became the key that unlocked a big part of what I call my Jolly-journey.

Legacy wealth intrigues me because there are elements of our lives that are, in a sense, hidden from our financial view. These dark places along our journey are hidden by gaps in our business (income) and financial (management) acumen. While they impact our pursuit of legacy wealth, we are blind to their measurable and meaningful existence. Navigating these dark places along our life's journey toward promise is the book's focus. I want you to see how you can get to where you believe your promise of legacy wealth resides.

Along my journey I have found we suffer from blindness when it comes to looking down the road financially. Our society has become a "right now" society. Waiting for things hoped for is not high on our priority lists, and as a result people no longer know how to build, grow, and expand things they really desire. This lack of long-term vision is so common, it's not even looked upon as blindness, more like bad luck, the system, or a wrong turn on a road of legacy. The group myth that the importance of connecting dots or passing torches is not something to focus one's life upon "results in an incapacity to bring attention to certain crucial aspects of our reality, leaving a gap in that beam of awareness which defines our world from moment to moment." Our world is a series of interconnected relationships with businesses, systems, finances, and cultures. These occur every day consciously and unconsciously. I want to raise awareness of this fact. I want to connect the ideas, dreams, missions, and collective purpose that span across generations so we can all journey this life seeing what we believe.

My journey helped me define the specific focus for the narrative of this book. That focus is to guide the way to notice what we do not notice—in other words, shine a glimpse of light in the dark places of our life journey. A "blind spot is a physiological metaphor for our failure to see things as they are in actuality. In physiology, the blind spot is the gap in our field of vision that results from the architecture of the eye." Ordinarily, what is missed by one eye is compensated for by the overlapping vision of the other. This is why we do not ordinarily notice our blind spots. When one eye is closed, the blind spot emerges. The blind spot in our individual and collective journeys are the closing of the doors between generations.

During my journey things were revealed to me as I spoke with thousands of people about faith, finance, legacy, wealth, and the Promised Land. The patterns in the responses that included elders, adults, and youth taught me how to fully observe present situations and understand that the dots must be connected between our past, present, and future to unearth the promises that reside in our personal lives, our legacies, and the business pursuit that resides within the two. I began to look for the patterns within the patterns, and right before my eyes a metapattern started to form.

Ten years later the metapattern I discovered has become a patent pending methodology called the NarrowRoad, a tool I use to guide individuals to their unique definition of the Promise in their own backyard. We often fail to see metapatterns because very few of us are taught to look for them. I have found that my grandmother is right: it is hard to see the full picture when you are posing for it. A method for getting outside yourself has become the key to extending the length of one's vision to that of legacy wealth.

My professional and academic training in finance, business, strategy, theology, and education has given me the ability to integrate varying types of perspectives and information. My research with pastors, other religious leaders, and our American history led me to see how the Promised Land was a sacred text that, regardless of your faith tradition, groups can organize around to pursue fruitful missions of promise. The levels and dimensions in one's relationship with money that appeared as the result of my research gave me confidence that finance, the stewardship of large sums of money both personal and collective was indeed a dark place along most everyone's journey. The contrasting viewpoints and opinions became evidence of a pattern that repeated across race, gender, class, and religious affiliation at each inflection point along the biblically narrated journey beyond the wilderness to the Promised Land. With each major degree of freedom—income, class, independence, and investment—there was a dark place needing the light of a torch that connected the past, present, and future pursuits of the promise of freedom. As I reflected and gathered more evidence, the pattern became more focused. The NarrowRoad is my metapattern. It is a journey of a series of decisions one must make concerning their faith and finance, one that details the promise hidden in between. This book strives to describe the pattern as clearly as possible.

Important Individuals along My Jolly-Journey

My cousin Dr. Benjamin Robinson III helped me first get on the road to a love and respect for institutional finance and banking. It was my father, the late Vincent Creswell Jolly Sr., who helped me narrow my road to pursue a path best suited for me to succeed. My inflection point came graduation weekend at Denny's over breakfast twenty years ago. My father would not let me leave the restaurant until I had finished my ten-year plan. It was 1994, and he wanted me to look further down the road to 2004. He would say, "I am proud of the steps you have taken thus far to begin a rewarding career, but it is always important to look further down the road early and make a plan to get there to not lose your way.

I see most things first in my mind, constantly researching facts and history for patterns to guide my clarity about problems I see in our community. Because I "think to see," it has been the classroom that gives me the most clarity. I have invested heavily in my ability to see through the acquisition of four degrees, and each degree heightened my awareness of the picture we all pose for. Hampton University gave me an appreciation for wisdom, collaboration and big vision, The Wharton School gave me a perspective of what it means to be set apart, think big, and invest in what you believe in. Boston University School of Theology gave me insight into the history of faith and the importance of owning one's theology, and the Graduate Theological Foundation allowed me to experience various schools of thought such as Oxford University's longstanding legacy of education and theology. In addition to all of these educational experiences I have read more than four thousand books to further refine my perspective of things such as business, finance, faith, strategy, American history, ethics, theology, women, men, purpose, and love.

My father had a saying: "The longer you are in school, the dumber you get." He used it to constantly challenge me with the question, "How are you going to translate all that education into something the average man can use?" The NarrowRoad is my attempt to deliver on his request. I want us all to understand that wealth is possible with a clear vision, proven thoughts, creative actions, and authentic speech.

The CEO of NationsBank, Hugh McColl, was a great teacher in demonstrating how wealth could be created via acquisition. Within thirteen years he had acquired more than fifty companies (including numerous banks) to create one of the largest commercial banks in the country. His ultimate desired outcome was to become the largest bank in America. I was able to see firsthand how he pursued his desired outcome during the four years I worked at NationsBank as an analyst, a commercial lender, and a VP in treasury management.

By 2000, I had graduated with my MBA and had accomplished my ten-year plan four years early and felt lost and unsure of my purpose. It was my mother, Sylvia Mae Horne Jolly, who then said, "You can make no mistakes if you take the time to think about your life, pray for direction, and believe—but keep it moving!" It was then I reached another inflection point, where I asked myself the same questions: What have I really accomplished so far? What do I still want to accomplish? What is my purpose? Where do I go here?

The inflection points of your life are where the road invites you to narrow it further—to get really specific about what you see and don't see, and what you really desire to understand, do, and express with others. In taking yet another inventory of my experiences and lessons learned, I came to realize key things I'd like to share with you. My hope is that perhaps in these pages we can both come away a little wealthier for the experience.

Did my dad know I would get to the end of my vision for the decade early? I found myself ten years ago at my second inflection point, ten years post that day in Denny's, I took a leap of faith and launched my own business, Torch Enterprises Inc. Torch stands for passing the torch from one generation to the next to build legacy wealth in our communities. It was a departure from the known and secure world of intrapreneurship to entrepreneurship. It was a road less traveled at that time for most of my peers, a road that narrowed my choices and forced me to devote most of my attention to finding answers to questions that had not been asked yet.

What I know from my journey thus far is that wealth is a group process. I learned this early, starting with my maternal grandmother stressing the importance of a savings account, having good burial insurance, a house you own, and money for the long term. It was further confirmed when I began my career as a banker, went to business school, started my business, worked in New Orleans post-Katrina, advised more than a thousand businesses, attended seminary, and conducted research for my doctorate studies.

Promises take time. Time to discern, time to create, time to build, time to grow, and time to expand to the next generation. My journey has revealed that Promises are more than worth the wait.

Introduction

Enter through the narrow gate. For wide is the gate and broad is the road that leads to destruction, and many enter through it. But small is the gate and narrow the road that leads to life and only a few find it.

— Matthew 7:13–14 (New International Version)

When the dots of the past, present, and future, are not connected, our legacies resemble that of "grasshoppers wandering in the wilderness" versus inheritors of the a Promise. This limited perspective of who we are across the time of generations can rob us of meaning, purpose, and identity. It works to dilute our understanding of how to leave inheritances that can create consistent wealth for generations to come—a core element of the journey to the Promised Land. Each successive generation must remember the promise for it to fully come into our possession. Life, when looked at in this way, provides each generation the opportunity to elevate their inherited standard of legacy to wealth however they define it. This way of looking at our lives is not unheard of, it is I have found, not consistent in our communities, as a result, many of us start from scratch leaving behind hidden treasure in our pursuit of wealth.

I have elected to use biblical and historical narratives of the Promised Land to unite the capitals of one's wealth identity with society's ongoing pursuit of the American Dream. The biblical narrative of the Promised Land is one that is familiar regardless of your faith tradition, race, or ethnicity largely due to Reverend Dr. Martin Luther King Jr.'s use of it during the march on Washington and throughout the Civil Rights movement. Fifty years ago, Dr. King declared he had seen the Promised Land and believed one day we would arrive at the place of promise where there is equality. His long-term vision was not equally shared amongst all who heard his declaration. Yet long-term vision is a requirement for declarations of independence, financial or otherwise, and often many at first are not in agreement with such declarations—yet the promise of the declaration still remains.

I wrote this book for five audiences:

- ☐ Visionaries who have the wisdom but not the knowledge of the resources necessary to build legacy wealth;
- ☐ Thinkers who have the knowledge but not the strategy and confidence to build legacy wealth;
- ☐ Doers who have the understanding of the work required to make money but not the understanding of the business around the work to create wealth for themselves;
- ☐ Speakers who have the passion and love for community, friends, and family but not the systems and structures to exchange and build wealth with those that matter most to them;
- ☐ Anyone who desires to be met where they are financially and guided to where they wish to go.

Why a Narrow Road?

We all seek direction in life, a way to go forward towards things we want most to happen. In my research I found that many young people are often frustrated with older generations because our elders are fond of telling them "what" they did in "their day" but often are light on the details of "how" they were able to reach such great heights and how their success could be replicated or even carried forward. I saw even in my own experiences with mentors who had broken barriers and surpassed what others thought was impossible, that detailing the specifics of "how" included aspects they did not want to share. This led me to understand that embedded in the explicit details of how to achieve success lie implicit elements of one's unique identity. These elements often get lost in translation and are as a result, left out of the stories we share to those who want to pick up our torch and move further down the road to yet another level of success. Imagine life as a highway that we are all traveling on, each of us enters on different generational ramps and take particular life choice lanes to get to our desired destination. Some of us go fast, some of us stay within the speed limit set by a governing official.

The Good News found in Matthew 7:14 speaks of a the wide gate of options we are presented in life. The text suggests a direction we are to go and it refers to a narrow road that leads to life that only a few find. When this text found me, it confirmed the road I was to take to present the work that leads to a life many want but few find completely. The NarrowRoad™ was created in direct response to the patterns of mistakes unconsciously made by well-intentioned, purpose-driven people like yourself when in pursuit of wealth via full ownership of your talents and opportunities that are presented to you along your life journey. These mistakes are what I refer to as dark places that link the distance between leaving and taking possession of an inheritance; mistakes that delay the passing of the torch of Promise from one generation to the next. Correcting these mistakes requires an in-depth understanding of faith and finance coupled with a willingness to explore the depth of who you are and where you desire to go in the window of time life gives you.

As the creator of this method, I believe that if more people were aware of their life purpose, their world as a result would become what was promised and our world would become more fruitful. With this increased level of awareness, navigating the inevitable financial wilderness to claim one's inheritance in the land of opportunity we live in today would be a necessary exercise to remember the legacy of what is important. We would become enlightened as to why you do not have to go the first leg of road alone; you have to go through the darkness of legacies that came before you to get to the light. Pursuit of the promise requires a solid foundation of knowing and believing that what is for you, is for you; it is promised. Lives before you were lived in pursuit of you getting further down the road.

Journeying through life in this way would in essence be along a narrow road, where a greater, more in-depth awareness of the legacy that fuels your life's purpose will enlighten your path through the wilderness. This legacy perspective is what makes the dark places lighter and more fertile for your life's mission. We want to spend less time wandering in the financial wilderness and more time unearthing hidden treasure we have inherited and already own. No more wasting time living from moment to moment or paycheck-to-paycheck, unaware of what has been passed on as your inheritance. The NarrowRoad method gives each of us a pathway to claim their inherited Promise and the tools to pass the torch for generations.

Collective change takes forty years. It marks the beginning and the end of an era. Living to see the Promise is possible when you connect as generations across the wilderness and know what to look for to pursue your individual life purpose. I have found that it is this level of knowing that is needed most to achieve the Promised Land defined according to your legacy.

Possession of a promise requires a vision, a strategy, a mission, a system of expression and defined outcomes. All of these factors together when combined with wise leadership and generational stewardship, finances the pursuit, creation, and ongoing operations needed to maintain the promise.

The reality of the biblical narrative is that once the Promised Land was acquired, the real journey began. "Finance is the allocation of assets and liabilities over time under conditions of certainty and uncertainty. A key point in finance is the time value of money, which states that a unit of currency today is worth more than the same unit of currency tomorrow." This is why we can't wait to focus on the pursuit of our Promise. Through the owning of your life assets, both inherited and created, you finance the pursuit of your Promise. In many ways, what I desire is a more perfect union between freedom and successful pathways in pursuit of it. It's interesting the patterned viewpoints my desire creates. Abraham in the Bible sought a more perfect union with God, President Lincoln sought a more perfect union between the north and the south, Dr. Martin Luther King Jr., a man who self-identified as a Moses, sought a more perfect union between America and her promise, and President Barack Obama declared this is a Joshua era and seeks a more perfect union between a black and white America and greater inclusion into the middle class.

Unity, agreement, and group decision are what brought on the ability for the Israelites to overcome their fear of giants in their land of promise. Unity is what brought on the victory of the North to overcome the resistance in the South. Unity is what forced America to see that segregation was not in alignment with her Promise. Finally it was unity that Americans needed to support the audacity to hope that there was change we could all believe in.

Within unity comes a movement toward another degree of freedom, and with each degree comes a different dimension of wealth. The metapattern of the NarrowRoad makes this plain for all who desire a unique pathway to life's promises. The NarrowRoad is a way to see what is not seen clearly about faith, finance, and the wealth that lies in between.

Freedom, as a result, is the ability to navigate beyond the financial wilderness and to choose to take possession of your promise, with the resources you have available in a manner designed by you.

Faith is a currency that connects what is to what is promised.

Wealth is a journey of a series of financial decisions that build and grow over time via savings and investments in what you understand and believe in.

Legacy is a narrative that did not start with you and will not end with you unless you discontinue the conversation across generations and stop passing the torch of wisdom, knowledge, and evolving understanding forward.

Legacy wealth is a journey to integrate the past, with the present to prepare for a future that our ancestors were promised. Legacy wealth is an individual pursuit of life purpose that rolls up into collaborative journeys that have generational, communal, national, and global implications.

The intricate design of America hinges on the belief that we are all one nation under God, a God who makes good on His promises. Within the melting pot of our collective congregation lies an abundance of hidden treasure, ideas, and dreams that have lost connection. It is our mission and purpose to call these dry bones together. Our pursuits of Promise depends on it. My research has made me confident of this fact. There is so much wealth that lies just beneath the surface of our current situations if only we had a way unite what it is we want and what it is we believe.

The pursuit of life, liberty, and ownership is not just the American Dream. These elements are contained in every journey. Starting with the Israelites and their pursuit of the Promised Land, to the Founding Fathers of America and their desire for a great nation, to the emancipated slaves and their desire for equity and ownership, which began with their pursuit of freedom. I believe there is no better time than now for us to get a clearer vision of the unique NarrowRoad that leads to the land we have been promised exactly the way we define it.

Your journey to the Promised Land in your life starts here. Promises, as you will come to understand, have dimensions. The road to Promise is narrow; it is unique for every individual. Not everyone will choose to go through each dimension of the Promise in their lifetime. This is why legacy narratives are so important. Letting your life speak to the values and victories of your pursuit is only half the story. The wealth you pursued and created along the narrow road of legacy wealth is a series of choices, and the extent to which you leave a legacy narrative helps those coming behind you to make similar if not better decisions to further the possession of yet another dimension of the promise.

This book guides you down a NarrowRoad to:

- ☐ Write your legacy wealth vision and anchor your life to it
- ☐ Take the time to make the vision plain and believe in it
- ☐ Address the dark places in your life that require necessary details to get beyond the patterns of the financial wilderness
- ☐ Face your fears so that your life speaks its truth
- ☐ Chart your path to legacy wealth along NarrowRoad designed by you.

There is an accompanying primer (at the end of key chapters) that begins to enlighten each journeyer along the NarrowRoad to see that legacy is wealth when considered as a long-term investment that spans generations. This book is an invitation to join a journey along the NarrowRoad to define and build wealth your way. The questions in the primer invite you to think strategically about phases of your life as independent pursuits of what you want in ways that will be effective in getting there. To accomplish your pursuits, do things "your way" according to your NarrowRoad Identity and you will find with a consistent budget of time you will navigate further down the road and out of the wilderness. Ultimately, this journey will assist you in igniting the hidden treasure inside you, shining the light for generations so that collectively we can show others with the realized promises of our lives, the reasons we can't wait to make legacy wealth a reality. The NarrowRoad helps journeyers clarify their purpose so life becomes more than income and expenses; it becomes a legacy that elevates its standard to wealth.

There are various roles we play along our life journey—visionary, thinker, doer, speaker, and a deliverer of outcomes (which we will discuss later).

Along the NarrowRoad everyone discovers their unique thought process. I am able to best process things through observations. As a result, my observations in the fields of financial services, strategy, investments, entrepreneurship, and theology have taught me tremendous things that build my confidence in what I do for a living. Being on the ground post-Katrina and in the boardrooms and conferences with both the wealthy and those who desire to be wealthy, have given me an advantage that I use in advising and strategizing for others.

My most preferred way to deliver outcomes is through partnerships. Similar to how Jesus sent the disciples out in twos, I can best deliver when paired with someone of complimentary expertise. This is why along the journey (should you choose to accept my invitation) you will be introduced to co-builders of solutions that can be custom tailored for you.

This may not make much sense to you now, but in the coming chapters you will come to know and hopefully love the dimensions of your NarrowRoad Identity (NRID) and ways it enriches your relationships with others, with money, with how you believe, and with your unique point of view. There are twenty-four unique identities within the NarrowRoad, and one is custom tailored for you.

Part 1: Our History

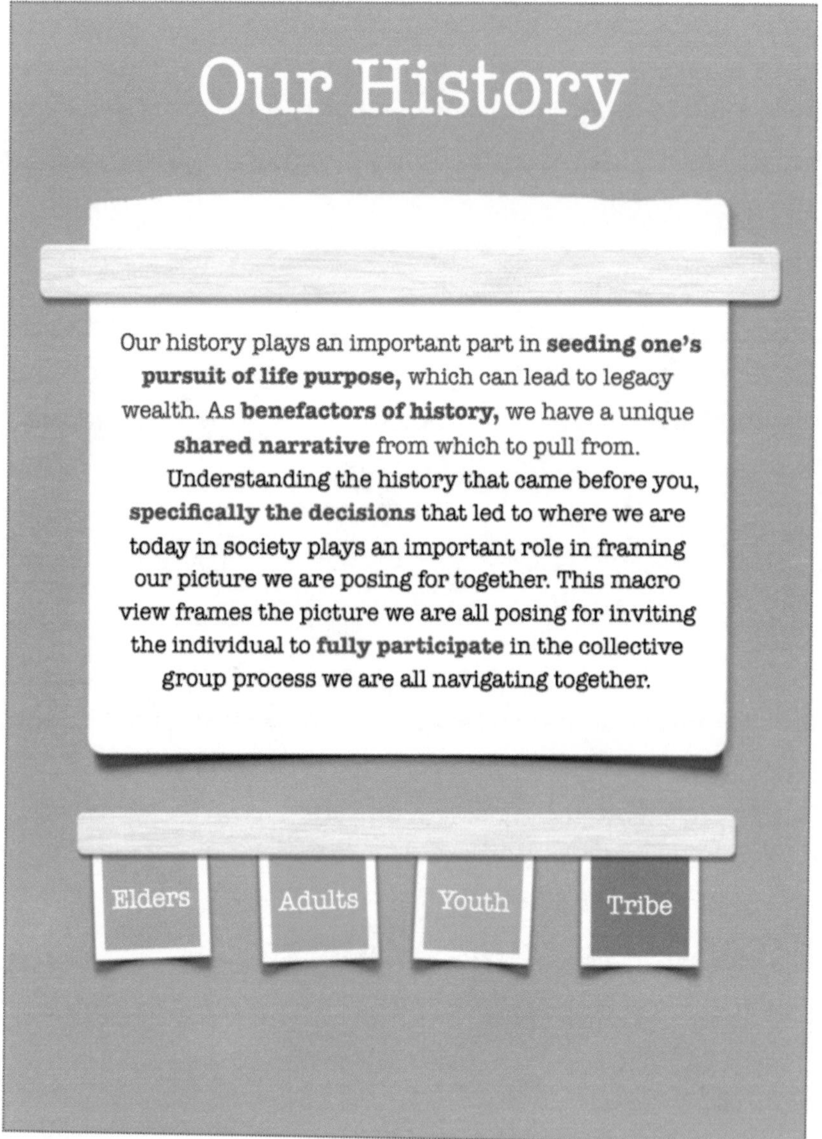

This book helps each reader to define a path toward legacy wealth by highlighting the relationship between your faith and your finance. Faith in this instance is complete trust or confidence in someone or something. That someone or something is entirely up to you and your theology. Finance in this instance is the stewardship of large amounts of capital, essentially the way you manage the stores of value within you (chapter 2), much of which is hidden lying buried underneath the cares of the world and your present definition of wealth creation.

Believing in something beyond yourself is essential to reach the heights that perhaps no one else in your family and or community has before. Your relationships with what lies between your faith and your finance once aligned with a clear vision of what wealth is for you gives you the power to build legacy wealth your way; which is the ultimate outcome of the NarrowRoad.

History serves as a context through which to ground the commonalities we as Americans all share in the pursuit of wealth. In the book The Fourth Turning by William Strauss and Neil Howe—the authors remark that "history once understood can be prophecy." Throughout my research journey I have seen this be true. We are all on individual and collective journeys in pursuit of the promise of a life lived as we desire. This has been and always will be.

The Fourth Turning is a masterful work that proves this theory by detailing Howe and Neil's research where they discovered that generations move in constellations called saculums, and every fourth generation repeats a cycle of life. Each generation's contribution to the ongoing narrative keeps the worlds wheel moving forward. Four generations make up a narrative that impacts a span of more than two hundred years. Four generations of ideas, dreams, missions, and lived purpose make up the world as we know it.

History can be prophecy if you take the time to see the patterns and believe. I reached out to the authors of the "Fourth Turning" while in New Orleans and shared with them my love for the book as well as the questions I had concerning the African American community. Five generations had lived in New Orleans and it was, after all, the oldest inhabited place in America—did that mean post-Katrina we were seeing the beginnings of a new turn of the wheel? I asked. Katrina was a sign of things to come, he said. Rebuilding post-Katrina would be fruitful for the journey that lies ahead of all Americans. He admitted that his research was not as vast on the history of African Americans and that it would be of great benefit to explore that history as I aimed to use his predictive model to chart a path for communities of color. I saw the history of African Americans as a useful prophetic guide for all Americans. The history of the African American journey is directly connected to the history of the business model of America. I saw then and believe now that the business condition of African Americans reflects on the business progress of America. Like it or not the pursuit of equality in America is consistently sparked by the legacy narrative of the Black community. This is a perspective you will learn along the NarrowRoad.

The conversation with Mr. Howe, however brief, left a definitive impression on me and as a result history of all types—American, biblical, African American, and business became the anchor from which every journey along the NarrowRoad begins.

Our founding fathers believed it was the providence of God that allowed them to forge together a declaration and a constitution that created one united nation. A nation of vast differences and one shared dream to build a nation under God that was democratic and free. In their belief system was the acknowledgement that there needed to be order, shared governance, and a commitment to wealth creation. In my travels through community after community I begin to ask myself, what knits us together? History. Business history was my answer. This nation is a business, a legacy business and we are all inheritors of its promise. The promise of business when pursued successfully is wealth. Wealth creation through ownership of the time, talent and subsequent treasure found in the field of opportunity called life. We share this history together yet few understand it completely. For history to be prophecy you much connect the dots of wisdom, knowledge, and understanding.

Chapter 1: Entering the NarrowRoad

When traveling along the NarrowRoad, here are some key things to remember.

Legacy and wealth are partners. Pursuing the NarrowRoad is how you will unite the two.

Faith, when unblinded financially, becomes a currency that reveals the abundant promise that exists for each and every one of us. Unblinded faith possesses both the substance and evidence of what you are hoping for.

Wealth is a journey whose narrative is a gift passed from one generation to the next to build opportunities via ownership.

Unity is the key to wealth; if you want to go fast, go alone, but if you want to go far, you must go together.

Wealth can be created in one generation and preserved in two. But it takes three generations to create legacy wealth, four generations to grow it, and five generations to expand it.

No matter what level of wealth you accomplish, it can all be lost in one generation—the link must continue; the torch must be passed. From the cross-section of experience and academic training I created the NarrowRoad, a unique system that integrates theology, finance, business, and unblinded faith into custom tailored curricula driven pathways for wealth building.

(Official White House Photo by Pete Souza)Public Domain. Additional source and credit info from the National Archives: Creator: U.S. Information Agency. Press and Publications Service. (ca. 1953 - ca. 1978) (Most Recent)

In 2008, I began asking the following question: If Rev. Dr. Martin Luther King Jr. self-identified as a Moses when he spoke of his dream of the Promised Land in 1968, and now, forty years later, presidential candidate Barack Obama began his campaign stating we are in a Joshua generation, and if this is our sociopolitical context, what is the Promised Land? How do we get there together? How do we fund the pursuit? And what, if anything, do you need to learn more of to feel more confident on your individual journey?

Within the theological underpinnings of the Israelites, the Promised Land was an inheritance they were to take possession of. Inheritance implies ownership and the invitation to build an enterprise that can sustain future generations outside the bonds of wandering in the wilderness and Egyptian slavery. Ownership is the possession of equity. This biblical narrative indicates that in the case of the Israelites, at the end of a long multigenerational journey, these emergent community builders only took possession of 10 percent of their inheritance. Similar to the notion that we humans only use 10 percent of our brainpower, there is so much more available to us if only we know how to take possession of it. The promise of wealth is no different.

Therein lies the primary lesson within a pursuit of a Promised Land. There is a need for connected understanding of how to take full possession of a promise. How does one link an idea of freedom to a promise of equality? What lies hidden in this question are the keys to wealth creation. Is it necessary to align your mission in life with an understanding of its purpose in relation to a promise that spans generations? Is this how we as individuals let our light shine? This is what I sought to uncover, with my "Jolly-journey" (see my name if you missed this reference)—a way for us to uniquely define ourselves so that collectively we could take possession of our promises by valuing each other. The keys I found along the road are embedded within what is now the NarrowRoad System. You unlock the keys to your promise once you go through the entry gate of the NarrowRoad, which reveals your wealth identity (NRID).

My business and personal experiences make it hard for me to imagine ownership without wealth. My academic training makes it difficult for me to consider faith without finance. The searching for a way to address the tensions that reside between the systems of business, and the structures of faith, ignited my prophetic imagination. I began to consider the sacred narrative of the Promised Land as a call to take possession of ancestral promises in our own backyard. Within the pursuit of the Promised Land resides a forty-year delay. My Jolly-journey erased my confusion about why we are waiting to pursue our Promised Land today.

Some of you may say, I don't know what she is talking about ... I'm pursuing my Promised Land, and I'm on my way.

To those of you who think this way, I say congratulations! Then I remember, according to the wisdom found in the biblical narrative of the Promised

Land, the pursuit was collective. We are supposed to go together. We navigate out of the wilderness in standards.

So where are our group processes? Who else is in your tribe? What is the specific area of your promise in the land? Which battles have you faced? Which ones have you overcome? How can each of us assist one another in taking full possession of each one's unique promise within this land we have in our midst? Is this unique to each of us?

Few people I interviewed associated the Promised Land with the opportunity to build a foundation for wealth creation. I look at everything through the lens of business. The primary objective of a business is to build wealth. In the democracy of America you are promised equal access to the pursuit of opportunities. Obtaining equality in America is your business, the path you choose to do it is your NarrowRoad to create.

Business can be defined as the practice of making one's living by engaging in commerce. Enterprise is a project or undertaking, typically one that is difficult or requires effort. For many, the practice of making a consistent living is an undertaking that is difficult or at least requires effort. Few people possess this perspective and even fewer apply business and financial principles to their pursuits of the Promise. As a result, the continuance of legacy wealth often gets lost in the financial wilderness due to the lack of understanding and faith in the importance of business and financial acumen. Essentially knowing how you go about your business is crucial to building wealth.

When one considers a lifetime of work, play, love, and faith, it takes time and money to pursue all of them. Yet few people I interviewed felt confident about their understanding of finance. The book of Proverbs 24:3–4 states that it is wisdom that builds the house but it is understanding through which it is established and made secure. Knowledge is what fills its rooms with rare and beautiful treasures—not surplus items from your local discount store. Knowing yourself, the choices unique to you, and the cost benefit of each are keys to building your house the way you see it.

My grandmother always says "time and land are the two things God is not making any more of, so steward both wisely." In the journey of our lives, are we doing that? Or is it just theory and not practice? Wisdom and not understanding? What I found was that there was a huge amount of mistrust of financial institutions, corporations, and even government, and mistrust often leads to miseducation. Miseducation, otherwise known as fear-infused doubt, leads to avoidance, and the avoidance leads to a similar position as the Israelites, who sat a three days journey away from their promise wandering in circles for forty years, afraid to face the giants in the land, feeling as if they were grasshoppers, incapable of defeating the great unknown in the uncharted territory that had been promised to their ancestors.

The Wealth Journey Continues

Similar to the Israelites, many of us who migrated in faith for freedom often fail to take full possession of our inheritances. In the African American community, the wealthiest segment alive today are often my grandparents' generation, who are now between their late seventies and early nineties. This generation, often born of sharecroppers, journeyed, marched, protested, and fought for the right to take possession of freedom. And for many, freedom was ownership. Yet many within this wealthy generation do not have either trusts or wills or systems for passing on an inheritance. My parents' generation are often asset rich but cash poor, which reduces their ability to buy these hard-earned assets out of probate when left unprotected to pass on to the next generation. Probate is a system of administering the estate of a deceased person that resolves all claims and ensures the distribution of the deceased person's property under a will. Ownership includes a responsibility of integrating systems of independence with systems of accountability, and for many there is a break across systems, which leads to a loss of hard-earned wealth.

A "grasshopper mentality" (see Numbers 13:33 King James Version), when faced with the giant decision of whether my legacy will be a wealth-creating business of permanence or a talent buried in the sand of legality, results in three generations of ownership failing to leave equity on the table that is needed for the next generation's advanced degree of freedom. Equity is a form of wealth, a form that too few really understand, so wealth is delayed for yet another forty-year period, and the wandering cycle in the wilderness begins again

What Does Wealth Mean to You?

Will you attain it in your lifetime? What is your relationship between faith and finance? What torch have you picked up to carry on further down the road of freedom? These are the questions that I launched my journey with some ten years ago. In seminary, I learned from Dr. Shawn Copeland that an argument is not a fight, it is a means to make something clear.

The Wealth Argument: Can we collectively get out of the financial wilderness?

The Wealth Problem: For most families and communities, the journey to legacy wealth is uncharted territory, and without a shared system for navigating the road to wealth in ways we can understand it is "hard to see the full picture when you are posing for it."

The Burning Wealth Question: Can individuals form wealth groups to corporately learn and build, grow and expand wealth that passes on for generations?

The Convincing Wealth Data: For many in America, business and finance are things to be avoided and mistrusted, yet for wealth builders they are the keys to designing a path toward multigenerational wealth creation and preservation, which can be used to make the world a heaven on earth, essentially better than we found it.

Building wealth is a long-term choice clouded amongst many short-term options that skip necessary steps required for wealth building. Each individual is in a position to build personal wealth, with their primary assets being their time, talent, and legacy perspective.

Personal wealth can lead to collective wealth, which can be used to support the needs of others. Businesses solve problems, and with so many problems in our communities, an ever-growing national debt, and city and state budgets failing, now is the time for more to understand how wealth and business are related and can be used to improve the world we live in.

The Persuasive Wealth Message: Legacy wealth is an intergenerational process of collective agreement and strategy. Commitment to the collective agreement must be renewed with each generation for it to continue in its development.

Wealth consists of a well-balanced portfolio of assets that includes human, intellectual, social, cultural, and spiritual capital. (Capital is a tool to support the building, growth, and expansion of wealth related activities. Pooled capital can expedite the process considerably.)

Wealth is a group process that integrates individual and collective values, perspectives, strategies, life missions, and outcomes. To build wealth, a group must agree to create a system that links the past to the present and the future in ways that honor and reflect both the ideas and intentions of every member of the group. The desired outcome of the wealth-building group must be the pursuit of legacy wealth however they define it. This will ensure that the commitment is not to an individual but to an outcome whose time has finally come.

The Persuasive Wealth Solution: Legacy wealth is a group process that can be created in three generations. The intergenerational wealth system must be embraced as a group agreement and anchored to a set of principles that reflect the unique legacy perspectives represented in the group.

The Negotiating Wealth Practice: Legacy wealth building is possible with the use of financial and business acumen to chart paths that successfully navigate beyond one's current financial situation to a path that leads to legacy wealth. Integrating strategy with the individual and collective goals and objectives is both qualitative and quantitative in practice.

The Wealth invitation: Let's journey together to understand a shared-legacy perspective that can unite us in our departure from the financial wilderness. Accept this invitation by igniting your flame with Torch Enterprises Inc. and making the NarrowRoad Guide your argument for legacy wealth creation.

Navigating Life Purpose through a Lens of Business

The purpose of the NarrowRoad is to chart a path toward one's life purpose inclusive of its financial aspects. We are all in some way builders of the future. Our present is the beginning of future generations' view of what is possible. After ten years of wandering in the financial wilderness looking for clues, my Jolly-journey is yet again shifting its perspective further down the road. The death of my father confirmed this shift. One of the last things he said to me was that "the legacy must continue." As I observe the current and recent graduates of both Hampton and Wharton, the parenting styles and professional pathways of my peers, parents, and grandparents I know we have what it takes to elevate the standard of our legacy to wealth. We just need a collective call and a road to pursue it. That is what you will find journeying along the NarrowRoad—an integrated, structured journey that infuses our history, legacy, business, systems, pursuits, and roadmaps to travel further down the road from income to savings to investments to wealth in ways that honor our legacy promise. Fifty years ago my ancestors, ancestors of this American nation, sang the promise that we shall one day overcome—in the case of the NarrowRoad, it is the overcoming of financial oppression.

Key Points to Note along the Road

Clarifying one's purpose begins by anchoring to an outcome you desire. Once anchored to an outcome, your purpose becomes manageable, more visible, and thus more of a promise than a possibility. What is it that you desire first and foremost?

Which of the following best describes your most immediate outcome?

I desire:

- ☐ **To move beyond survival,** no more living from paycheck to paycheck
- ☐ **To define freedom for me** by living a lifestyle I can comfortably manage and enjoy
- ☐ **To move beyond socially accepted freedom** and grow to a level of financial independence
- ☐ **To plan how best to leave wealth** that expands my legacy wealth narrative for generations

Legacy is a cross-generational narrative—we are all in someway connected. Each of the outcomes listed above relies on the one before it and after it to succeed. To move beyond survival, one must earn more income than one spends, which requires greater consumption from those who are free to create the need for more income earning opportunities. To move beyond freedom, one must learn how to save and invest in opportunities that are created by those who are planning long term for the not-so-plainly-seen future. To leave wealth that passes on for generations, one must be able to see the opportunities in all the dimensions of wealth evolving along the way, following in the footsteps of those who came before us and are coming after us.

Wealth creation, when viewed along your NarrowRoad, is a series of financial decisions that build, grow, and expand over time with savings, ownership, and investments. Your wealth journey contains options, decisions, and choices you must make to get where you desire to go. Many of us need a roadmap to clearly see the road we are on to determine if it is the best road to take. It starts with anchoring the end of your current situation to an outcome listed above.

Assignment—Entering the NarrowRoad

The NarrowRoad is a patent-pending business system. The uniqueness of the NarrowRoad System is its ability to become custom tailored to you and your current financial situation with the answer to one simple "Entry Gate" question. You are invited to enter the NarrowRoad at the beginning of this book to tailor your journey as you read through the chapters. The book, when read this way, allows you to journey with each chapter as you see fit.

To enter the NarrowRoad, please answer the following entry-gate question. You can do this one of two ways:

4. Visit www.mynarrowroad.com/entrygate and listen to the guided meditation that will help you reveal your NarrowRoad ID.

5. Uncover your NRID with this manual process: take a moment and close your eyes, take a few deep breaths, and turn off your mind and emotions. Take a few more breaths and travel down to the core of who you are. Anchor yourself to the source of your inner confidence, the place where your inner voice speaks. Once peacefully there, I want you to answer the following question without thinking or feeling. Answer from the inner knowing within you: There are four roles: visionary, thinker, doer, and speaker. What is your strongest role, second strongest role, third role, and fourth role? Write them down as they come to you. Trust what you hear. Place your responses below on the left, and then match up each role with the appropriate number on the right

Place your response to the entry gate question here:

Rank each role #1- #4 Strongest – Weakest	
RANK ORDER	ROLES
	THINKER
	DOER
	VISIONARY
	SPEAKER

Doer	Speaker
#3	#4
#2	#1
Thinker	Visionary

The NarrowRoad™ Entry Gate

Congratulations! You have officially entered the NarrowRoad. The purpose of the NarrowRoad is to assist fellow journeyers to chart a path toward one's life purpose, to build a roadmap for your life business to ensure that where you are headed is in the direction you ultimately desire to go. The belief is that anchoring to a wealth outcome helps clarify your purpose and narrows your focus to the steps that with faith you will take to attain it.

Anchoring to an outcome you desire also makes it easier to navigate through the financial wilderness of life. Remember, life is all about stewardship—stewardship of your time, talent, and treasure in ways that multiply your opportunity to grow. Stewardship is what finance really is—stewardship of vast amounts of capital you possess and have access to. When you look at your life as a whole, you go from your father's seed that was harvested by your mother and invested in by your "family business," to a creator of wealth for others throughout your career, to hopefully a creator of wealth for yourself along the way, and finally to an investor in future generations. If the average career span is forty years, we are all in our very own unique ways million-dollar businesses. We are all servants with talents, but some of us are burying a host of these talents in the sands of illiteracy, confusion, chaos, and doubt. It's time to master the art of our personal business so that individually and collectively we can create a life of purpose and promise.

Wealth, after all, is a group process. Find your group, exchange within it, and you can build your wealth. The Promised Land is a familiar narrative that shines light on the reality of a purpose-driven life. Our families are links to a pursuit of promise that is defined in unique ways that continue to grow and expand with the choices we make and risks we take. A promise is something you must pursue and then take possession of. To take possession, you must believe that the time and risks involved in pursuing it are worth it.

I believe there are many promises buried in the sands of history, forgotten legacies due to fear, chaos, confusion, and doubt. But a promise is for an appointed time. All one has to do is connect, anchor, remember, believe, and pursue. So let's take some time to find the necessary elements to once again believe in promises.

Rules of the Road

Legacy is a cross-generational narrative. It is an ongoing dialog about what is important when considering the question of where we go from here. Everyone in their own way wants to know what is going to happen next. That question "where do I go from here?" remains the link that connects our generations.

History can be prophesy if you take the time to remember to connect the dots between the past, the present, and the future.

The legacy narrative with each generation can be elevated to a new standard, a new way of leading, investing in the future. It is in this way the narrative can be elevated to include wealth if you connect the ideas and dreams across generations.

Within the connections, you will learn there is a storehouse of hidden treasure waiting for you to fuel your pursuit.

Wealth is a series of financial decisions that build, grow, and expand over time with savings and investments. The higher your level of acumen, the greater your opportunity for wealth. Wealth comes with ownership of your vision, thoughts, actions, and voice.

As a result, legacy wealth is a journey that connects you with the past, present, and future. It is a promise that everyone has access to.

You alone must chart your path to take possession of it. Your choices narrow your road. Once on the road, you find like minds and hearts to create, build, partner, and align with along the way.

Our elders are right when they say, "What is for you is for you." I translate that to mean that wide is the gate of life, and narrow is the road of your purpose within it. Few take the time to find their purpose and even fewer take the road that leads to it. I believe the few who take it have learned the importance of remaining connected to the legacy narrative and picking up the torch to take it even further down the road. Living a life in this manner opens doors of opportunity that are not readily available to everyone, just to those who know the pathway to their treasure hidden in the dark, fertile areas of their legacy.

Chapter 2: A Portfolio of Talents

What happens to a dream deferred?
Does it dry up
like a raisin in the sun?
Or fester like a sore—
And then run?
Does it stink like rotten meat?
Or crust and sugar over—
like a syrupy sweet?
Maybe it just sags
like a heavy load.
Or does it explode?

— Langston Hughes, "A Dream Deferred"

What is your dream?

We all have dreams, snapshots of the future that with a little faith in something will come to fruition, what is yours? Have you ever taken the time to cost out your dream? Think through what it is going to take in terms of time, talent and treasure? Because all dreams require the investment of these three. Every dream in someway is financed with people's time.

My dream is that anyone and everyone who desires to live life more abundantly learn the best method to do so. A dream I have learned will only get you so far down the road, there is more to the journey to bring it into reality. Some dreams take generations to come true, some happen in an instant. A dream fulfilled brings wealth to all who took the time to believe in it, wealth in this instance is the ability to bear fruit in places some never knew existed. The faith part of a dream is belief in something beyond yourself. While it is true that '78 percent of America associates themselves with some form of Christian Faith Tradition', beyond that statistical fact my research revealed that just about everyone when faced with a financial challenge or confusing situation simply closes their eyes and believes in something. A dream of the future as a result has within in it both faith and finance.

Within your hands rests a wealth-navigation tool committed to meeting you where you are and guiding you however far down the road of wealth you desire to travel. The accompanying summary primer (located at the end of each chapter) is designed so that once you understand the NarrowRoad and its principles, you can begin the journey and chart a path toward legacy wealth of your very own. The ultimate destination of the NarrowRoad is legacy wealth for you and your community—however you define it. The five facets of the definition of legacy wealth is what we will explore in each chapter of book. You will come to own a personal definition for yourself that you can pass onto future generations as you continue to navigate further down the road. Why is this important? Along my research journey I found that the distance between the elder generations knowledge of what to do and the younger rising generations desire to do is a little word "how." Younger people are not satisfied with what you did, or even why you did it, for them to believe they can pick up the torch and carry the dream forward they need to understand how. And that often gets lost in translation and faded memory of the story.

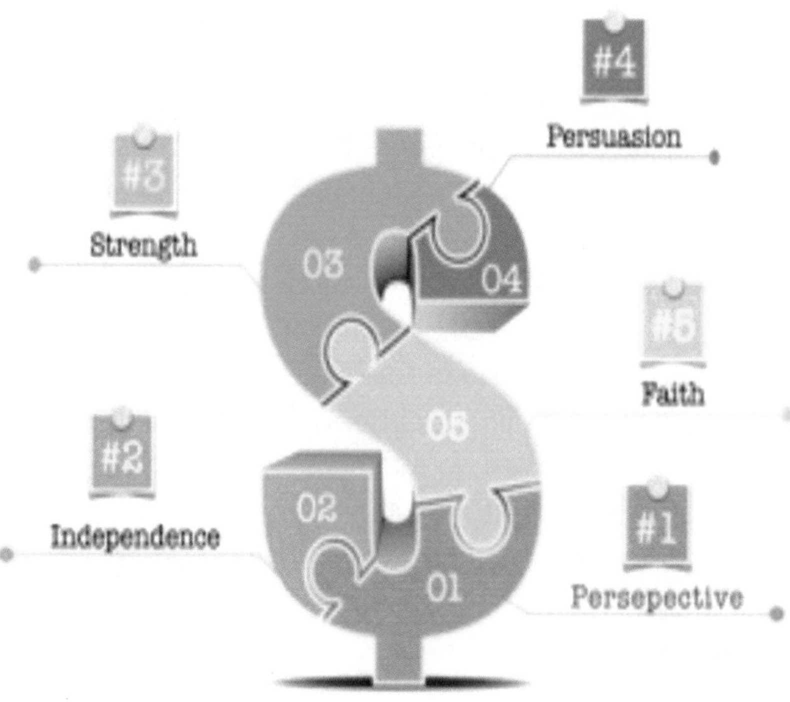

Mynarrowroad.com/talentinventory

Everyone Is Born with a Portfolio of Talents

Like capital, talent comes in various forms. Invested capital is equity, and when one has equity one has shares of ownership of something valuable. When one decides to pursue legacy wealth, there are stores of treasure hidden in places you have not eyes to see yet, buried in the depth of who you are. Your life is a snapshot of how wealth is created. It contains the hopes and dreams of generations past coming to fruition. Your lifestyle as a result creates wealth and sends messages for all the world to hear and ultimately see. Your life is a message that speaks more truth than many of us realize.

Your purpose is to uncover the true message you are here to share. Messages are like systems: they integrate ideas, dreams, missions, and promises into collective exchanges people can feel and believe in.

This book invites you to let your life speak its truest purpose, the innermost desires of your heart. Chart a path to fulfillment of your truth, what you desire most for yourself, your community, our world, your legacy. Arrival at purpose cannot help but produce wealth. Every seed that reaches fertile ground is promised to reap a harvest. The NarrowRoad helps chart a clear path to the harvests of you.

Some of us are blessed enough to arrive at inflection points in life when we can take a moment, reflect on our life, and say, "My life is amazing. It's fun, relevant, and I believe I am making a difference—I could continue along this road for the rest of my life." This is where the road has narrowed to a point of purpose; your life is speaking your truth, and your heart has found its desires and peace.

For most of us, a life such as the one described require big changes to take place, the road is still very wide and we need a strategy to narrow our focus and find some direction. Big change only happens when people can afford to see that change is necessary—only when people can see and understand the financial implications of shifting their perspective further down the road can the business of their lives reflect their hopes and dreams. Focusing on the now is not only easy its comfortable. For most, thoughts about the future are left up to faith, hope, and a dream. These are the driving forces that impact the business of the majority of our communities.

There are billions of people on the planet who need a way to better understand finance and business on a level that matters—their own. What I have learned is that the financial system is like all systems: largely neutral—it is the people who bias it. And so the big change that is needed to improve the financial systems at work in our lives and communities is a greater level of conscious participation. To unblind the faith that surrounds our finances and become more aware of the unconscious consumption that fuels our hopes and dreams, we must write our legacy wealth vision and make it plain and then learn how to use our talents to make it happen. This starts with a budget, a plan on how you are going to spend your time with your talents that grows into a financial plan that includes strategic investments and of course savings.

I know this sounds more than familiar, it's basic common sense. My question is are these things a consistent part of your daily lives, my research showed that for many of us the answer is no. As a result of this, I am suggesting that we elevate our standard of business. A standard meaning a required or agreed level of quality or attainment. Something we share and talk about with those who matter most. Imagine what will happen when standard of business shifts from an income focus of day-to-day work to that of legacy wealth investments that span decades and generations. With the advent of social media and technology, the ability to come together in more ways than social are a compelling enough argument to spark the big change that is both desired and needed. The issues we face in our community are handled financially, everything costs, and requires an investment of some kind. Our standard of business must shift from an income focus of day to day to that of legacy wealth of decades and generations. With the advent of social media and technology, the ability to come together in more ways than social are a compelling enough argument to spark the big change that is both desired and needed. With the approval by the SEC for Crowd-equity funding_, referred to as Title III under the Obama Administration's Jobs Act, there is an increasing need or all of us to become more fiscally responsible and aware of the principles of business and financial acumen. Investing in businesses upon final approval of Title III will become an opportunity that includes non accredited investors. Non-accredited investors will have the option to include investing in businesses in their wealth creation strategy. This will require a solid foundation of business and financial acumen to make the right choices for your desired level of wealth creation. There are risks involved that you must be aware of and feel confident about pursuing.

Essentially, the change is an elevation of perspective beyond a focus on now to further down the road—to our future, the continuation of history, the building of a legacy. This is where and when life as we know it in our communities can get very exciting.

Can we collectively get out of the financial wilderness? Yes, we can. The way, while simple, is not easy when attempted alone.

The Talents in Your Portfolio

Your ability to see, think, do, speak, and arrive at outcomes in a way that is unique to you. Cultivating connections between wisdom knowledge and understanding is the key to successful management of your wealth portfolio.

Two Bible verses set the context for the raison d'être of the NarrowRoad:

Proverbs 2:6: "For the LORD giveth wisdom: out of his mouth cometh knowledge and understanding" (King James Version).

Proverbs 24–4: "By wisdom a house is built, and through understanding it is established; through knowledge its rooms are filled with rare and beautiful treasures" (New International Version).

One of the key first steps in building wealth is getting your financial house in order. How you accomplish this is through the wisdom of those that came before you. Your introduction to business occurred in your childhood. It was here your house was established. How did you grow up with money, value, leadership, confidence? In my research what I found was that two generations ago, when our grandparents where seeding, building, growing, and expanding the world as we know it today, many of them believed God that "one day" it would all be ok. When you go back four generations (if you can) all they had was God to put their minds at ease. The way you grew up with money is a continuation of those faith filled beliefs.

"By wisdom a house is built"

From this foundation of wisdom you choose to how to create your own financial house that you will order. Your current financial situation reveals how much wisdom lies in your houses foundation. Establishing a financial house requires the use of all five of your capitals. The more wisdom you deploy the more capital you allocate toward creating the assets you need to establish yourself. Cracks in your foundational wisdom show up as inconsistencies in your understanding of how wealth is created. This is not a permanent problem this is just a current situation that your NRID will help you get beyond.

"From this foundation of wisdom you choose to how to create your own financial pursuit"

Knowledge of self is how you exit the financial wilderness. By taking the time to know what it is you desire to do with your life, how best to pursue your desires, and how to ask for help when you need it is how you build the confidence to believe in your dreams and take responsibility for your mission once you choose to accept it.

"Through understanding it is established"

To establish a house you must build walls. Walls are decisions, choices you must make along the road to wealth. They govern your roadmap and help design your pursuit out of the financial wilderness. Knowledge is different from education. Education is what you buy; knowledge is what you own. It is education applied to a confidence level of acumen. This is the type of knowledge required for executing decisions focused on taking possession of the promise of legacy wealth in your life.

Your history and our history can become prophecy when viewed in this way.

Chapter 3: Life, Liberty, and the Pursuit …

That all men are by nature equally free and independent and have certain inherent rights, of which, when they enter into a state of society, they cannot, by any compact, deprive or divest their posterity; namely, the enjoyment of life and liberty, with the means of acquiring and possessing property, and pursuing and obtaining happiness and safety.

— Virginia Declaration of Rights _

The idea of entrepreneurship and its role in the next chapter of our American future is an interesting one to consider. For those of us yet to enter the degree of freedom we desire, entrepreneurship could perhaps be a road worth considering. This road, both challenging and rewarding, is one that requires great planning and determination. I myself have been in the pursuit of ownership for the past eleven years, and have found that history is an entrepreneur's best teacher.

Within the Declaration of Independence rests a well-known phrase: "Life, liberty, and the pursuit of happiness" is considered by some as part of one of the most well-crafted, influential sentences in the history of the English language. The phrase is meant to exemplify the "inalienable rights" with which all human beings are endowed by their Creator and for the protection of which they institute governments.

Originally penned by George Mason, this phrase and its derivatives, known as the Mason Concept, "became living law in every American constitution and is now in every world constitution except those of Russia, Mongolia, Ukraine, and Guatemala." As the Mason Concept traveled along the lane, whispers substituted the doctrine of equality of birth, for the common-sense doctrine of equality of freedom and independence. The whisperers also substituted a vague "pursuit of happiness" for the ownership of property and attainment of happiness.

Here is the original as it was written by Mason: "That all men are born equally free and independent, and have certain inherent natural rights, of which they cannot, by any compact, deprive, or divest their posterity; among which are the enjoyment of life and liberty, with the means of acquiring and possessing property, and pursuing and obtaining happiness and safety."

George Mason was very nearly considered a prophet. In his ample library at Gunston Hall, he had filtered five thousand years of history to create the principles of the Virginia Declaration of Rights that were the distilled essence of history's bitter fruits gathered from her attempts at happiness. George Mason was a delegate to the Constitution Convention in Philadelphia in 1787. He refused to sign a proposed Constitution that sanctioned human slavery and omitted the rights of men. The first six words of his Objections were heard in every hovel and on every frontier of America: "There is no Declaration of Rights!" He carried his deathless struggle for a Federal Bill of Rights to the people, and lived barely long enough to see his efforts crowned with victory and his name drowned in oblivion, because of the bitterness engendered in that struggle. This was his life's work, his liberty and his pursuit. His legacy of ownership lives on today as the fundamental fiber of the world's constitution.

Without attainment, the pursuit of happiness can be costly and painful. Happiness and safety may not be obtained in this world without "the means of acquiring and possessing property." For some reason this association was discarded for a more general phrasing, leaving most of us business illiterate to the relationship between pursuit of happiness and the pursuit of ownership. And the whisper continues. Ownership is becoming lost in the affordability shuffle, and with it wealth becomes a tagline for those who own what most consider more useful to rent.

Root Meanings

I would like to take you on a journey that explores the root meanings of life, liberty and its pursuits through a business interpretation. Why? Because I believe that understanding the material details that lie underneath what it means to be an American in the pursuit of happiness is important for those desiring to be financially independent. My research study along my journey to building the NarrowRoad included the topics of faith and finance. What I found most interesting is the levels of chaos and confusion people have about the value of being an American and the profitability one can attain by executing their rights.

To believe that the creation of wealth will be the outcome of your pursuit in life, is a choice. Once chosen, life becomes a very narrow road. The ancient path of business is 80 percent the same, leaving only 20 percent of the route you take up to you and your unique difference. Creativity does play a part in the success of your business pursuit; however it is the fundamentals that are required to see it through beyond your vision to the thoughts, actions, and desires of others. Those who travel along their narrow road to successful pursuits find few opportunities to look to the left or the right for a glimpse of what is along the sidelines threatening to overtake them; they sincerely focus on the change that is to come from their focus on declaring their independence.

What I have found is that successful pursuers focus on the road straight ahead with expectation the road will lead to the upward climb of achievement and profitability. The gate to entrepreneurship is wide, and filled with plenty of options and distractions; the narrow road is the way of experience, yours or that of others that have come before you. My travels have led me to understand the light of proven experience is never shed upon idea-generated whims unless you are repeating the same leap of blind faith over and over again.

Ideas to true entrepreneurs are but stepping-stones to a better view of how dreams can become materialized visions; all of which are required to live a life focused on attaining liberty and happiness. Happiness, remember is literally ownership if you take the time to learn from our history.

One of the reasons entrepreneurship is often avoided is because it is at first hard to find success. Owning the definition of entrepreneur is essential to attaining its potential success—different from a business owner, an entrepreneur owns and operates various businesses taking on an enormous amount of risk to do so. Imagine with me the concept that anyone working, living and exchanging with others, growing and expanding their family legacy footprint, and balancing all of that on a budget is in their own way an entrepreneur. The path entrepreneur's first navigate is one of thorny ground, filled with challenges to prove that what appears to themselves can in fact be a dream for others to follow. Success for the entrepreneur comes from the pruning of thorns that are not actual priorities for the milestone at hand. Fundamentals in this stage of risk development are bounded by the fundamental 80 percent of business. Declarations are patterned when independence is the pursuit.

Key Lessons for the Pursuit

An understanding of what I will call the legacy thread is what I have found assists people focused on financial independence via ownership. This legacy thread connects the core elements of America's business model. This thread is like a three-stranded cord that if well intertwined, cannot be broken, and has a history of leading groups of Americans to wealth-bearing success. To some groups of Americans, the strands of this cord have been tightly wound together for generations; it has become a tradition that enables each generation to pursue greater degrees of freedom—financial and otherwise. For other groups, the cords are not yet attached, in contrast the strands lie separated like dry bones in a dark valley, reducing their pursuits to short-lived phases of promise that fizzle shortly after the spark of an idea, or season of consistent income. The following illustration desires to provide a glimpse into what is needed to link the three strands together so that you can find the value promised in the history of the pursuits of declared financial independence.

Strand One: Life

Life is a gift. But what type of gift? For me it's a gift that if paid attention to, keeps on giving. In essence it multiplies or appreciates over time. Looking up the word life in the dictionary will give you varied answers, such as: the capacity for growth, reproduction, functional activity, and continual change all the way until you die. Put another way, it is your eighty-plus-year potential to create, leave an impact, or contribute to the current situation as you see it.

Seen through the lens of business, life to me is an asset—not just for you but also for the benefit of others.

Yet lives often it go underutilized, undeveloped, underestimated and over-leveraged. Some life is often limited to transactions based on the now required activities. In this case, life is only valued through the lens of money, which seems more to me like a path of hustle than a path leading toward legacy wealth.

Life, if not taken care of (despite the body's functional potential to self-heal and one's intellectual and emotional capacity to reach great heights) can depreciate rapidly by incurring liabilities (such disease and the cost of health care, and fear based decisions) which could deplete the useful ability of your life asset. (This makes simple choices like fast food look like a debit to your balance sheet, in my opinion). Essentially, life is an asset whose value is determined by its shareholder (that's you).

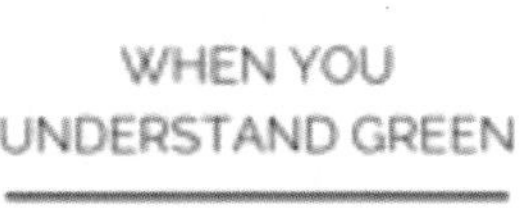

Strand Two: Liberty

Liberty is something some people take very seriously. For instance, recall the phrase: "Give me liberty or give me death!," a quotation attributed to Patrick Henry from a speech he made to the Virginia Convention on March 23, 1775, at St. John's Church in Richmond, Virginia, and is credited with having swung the balance in convincing the Virginia House of Burgesses to pass a resolution delivering the Virginia troops to the Revolutionary War. Among the delegates to the convention were future US presidents Thomas Jefferson and George Washington. Reportedly, those in attendance, upon hearing the speech, shouted, "Give me liberty or give me death!"

For those of us not so dramatically inclined, liberty can mean the power or scope to act as one pleases; in other words, your ability to see what you want and choose to make it happen, whichever way you deem appropriate or can afford with your life asset. Liberty for me is one's ability to see and invest in the change you want to happen now, the right to rebel or support the status quo. You own this right. The fight for liberty is a longstanding pattern in the history of the American people. Looking at it through a business lens, liberty is the equity you own and are willing to invest for the right change or cause you believe in.

Exploring the first two threads have uncovered assets, liabilities and owner's equity. When history is looked upon in this way one's balance sheet can be found in the field when life and liberty are appropriately valued and invested.

OWNERSHIP

IS HOW YOU TAKE POSSESSION OF THE PROMISE

PURSUIT OF IT REQUIRES YOUR HOUSE & YOUR LEGACY BUSINESS TO BE IN ORDER

Strand Three: Pursuit of ...

I leave the place after "of" blank because happiness is subjective—meaning uniquely defined by you. Pursuit means by definition: to strive toward, to quest after or for, to search for. It can also mean: an aim, goal, or objective, a dream. To pursue something is to continually strive to arrive at ways to maximize your capacity. To pursue can also mean to build upon a glimpse of what is possible and remain consistent to see it through until fruition. Pursuit in this case is similar to an operating system of actions and strategies anchored to a specific goal and objective. For me, one's pursuit is how a person actualizes their dream or monetizes their business with assets they have at their disposal. The object of the pursuit though ownership one derives a profit, and by achieving that milestone, overcoming the hurdles to so, you move beyond the limitation of starting from scratch generation after generation. Thus your pursuit can be an income statement of how to arrive at sowing the seed of your vision (top line revenue) and reaping its harvest (bottom line profit/success) of your business. The pursuit is taking ownership of whatever you deem is the way to master a successful route to wealth however you define it.

Linking the Strands

The glue that links these strands together is happiness or, as George Mason, the author of the premise of American freedom, stated: ownership. Happiness in America is largely based on the ownership of something. In the beginning days of America, you could not vote if you did not own property. This is still pretty much the way it is today; the largest owners of assets have greater influence than those who wander in the wilderness of financial management often because they can afford it.

As stated before, happiness is subjective when left to the eyes of the beholder, and is often reduced to just a mental or emotional state of well-being. It is often characterized by positive or pleasant emotions, ranging from contentment to intense joy. In our current framework, happiness could be related to the condition of your business and in the ways in which you optimize the use of your assets and the investment of your equity through the operations of your system of pursuit. Done well, happiness would then equate to joy throughout the process. It is here where this strand of declared independence gets interesting.

In a world where there is the seen (which is the "already done") and the unseen (which is the "not yet manifested"), both life and business include lives, liberties, and pursuits. At this inflection point it is the entrepreneur who answers the question: Where do we go from here? It is the successful owner who sets the destination of the pursuit.

What underlies the definition of freedom and happiness in America is a confusion of what financial happiness really means. For the American business model, happiness is increased levels of ownership in the business of success. The cost of ownership in the American business model is taxes (property, income, sales, and for some, estate). The benefit is that when executed correctly the owner gets to create what otherwise would remain unseen. Only you know what happiness financially means to you. Prayerfully you have budgeted for it. If not I encourage you to chart a path along the NarrowRoad a budget is not a set of limits it is a plan for executed choices, decisions you have agreed to commit your five sources of capital resources.

So one might argue that the level of happiness or freedom depends on the level of ownership. From a distance, the current discourse in America stems around the ownership levels of the 99 percent and 1 percent. Up close through a distorted business lens, it can be confusing how wealth is created and who should bear the burden of the cost of freedom in America. Again this largely boils down to ownership, which is a form of entrepreneurship. I lived long enough to believe that systems are neutral; it's the people that are biased. Perhaps if more people participated in the system of ownership, the bias as it currently resides could and would eventually change to a more balanced view, one that is more representative and understanding of both the value of hard work and the value of owning at least some part of business around the work. If America is the land of the free, and you feel you are not, what specifically is stopping you—is it the system or your lack of understanding of a way to bias the system in your favor? Perhaps unemployment or underemployment viewed in this way could be an invitation to declare your pursuit of independence. Essentially own your system for success and build wealth your way.

As we all reflect on our collective right to vote, I encourage you to take the time to review what is it that you desire to own with your gift of life. What liberties does that require you to take? And in the light of these two strands, what does this mean for the direction of your pursuit? Be sure to invest the time to fully understand your position. It is after all your right to pursue it here in America and be successful. The choice always remains with you and what you desire to do with your capitals to build legacy wealth.

Legacy Is More than an Idea: a Lifelong Pursuit

An entrepreneur is more than someone with an idea and a slick marketing way to spin it. He or she takes on greater than normal financial risks in order organize and operate a business that changes things. A true entrepreneur is someone who has the wisdom, knowledge, and understanding to braid the threads of the cord that ground our American Dream together. An entrepreneur along the NarrowRoad is any individual who owns a way to create a future we all can take possession in; whether they be a consumer, investor, employee, co-founder, successor, or inheritor.

For me, becoming an entrepreneur is a call. Have you been called? What is it asking of you? The 80 percent of the call is asking you to take the time to value your assets, own your equity, rev up your operations, and define happiness in whatever way you desire to own it. It is also asking you to remember to pay your taxes so that the America as we all know it will continue its journey to mirror the happiness we all in someway desire to pursue. I am thankful for what this journey has revealed about the business model of America and its need for more of us to actively participate in it. I pray you find happiness in this revelation too.

Regardless of the risk of your call, and the resulting influence it has on your pursuit, stay blessed and continue the journey. Remember, wide is the gate of opportunity; narrow is the road to its success. May you be one of the increasing few who find it and chose to pursue it with ownership and every ounce of equity you have within you. From my perspective, if you do, then the best is surely yet to come.

Part 2: Our Legacy Narrative

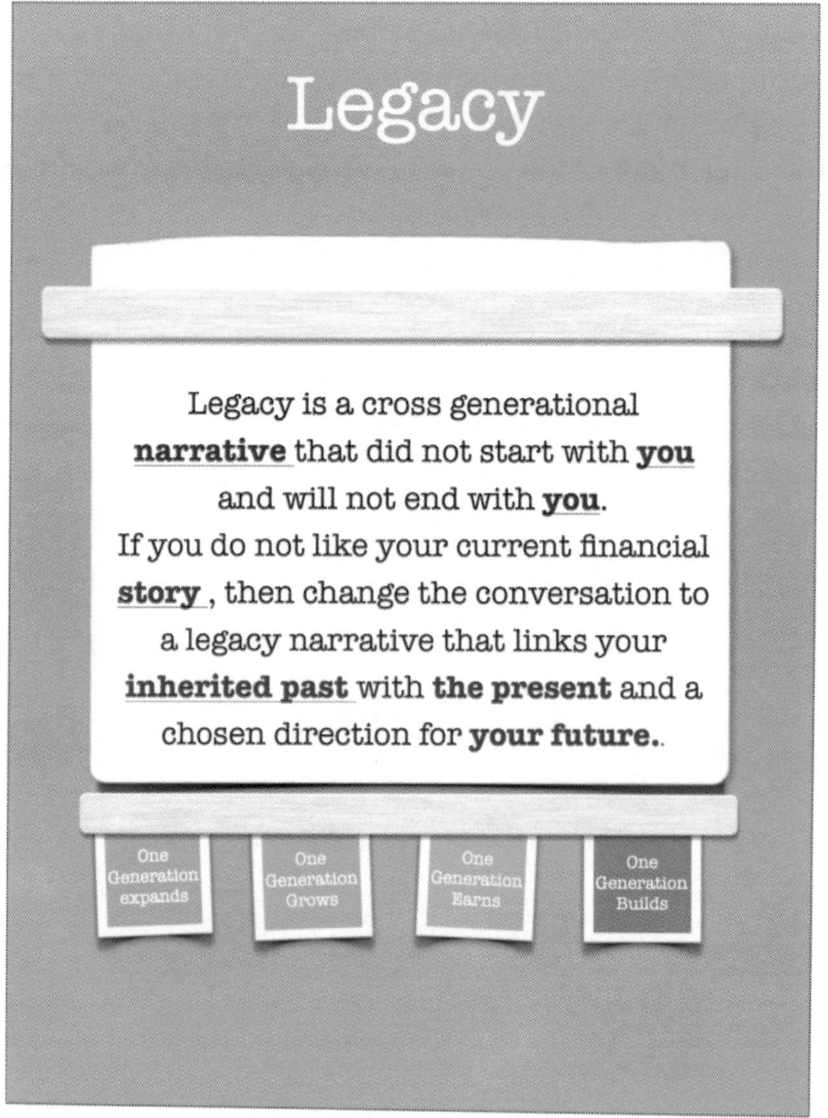

Chapter 4: Weathering the Storm

Nothing happens until something moves.

— Albert Einstein

Along the NarrowRoad a storm occurs when you live leaning entirely on your own understanding, believing you can do it all. While armed with good intentions, eventually you find out you have not a clue as to how it will all get done in your lifetime. This leads to avoidance of critical things that are easier to face when you are not tackling everything on your own.

When in the storm there are what I call pain points that can burden you with more than you can handle by yourself. Something has to move for you to get out of the storm and that normally is your willingness to become vulnerable to the reality that teamwork is what really makes our dreams work. Wealth really is a group process. Collaborations really do build a future more in line with the desires of your heart. Make that team a cross generational one and you are on the road to legacy wealth.

I am blessed to be able to speak across the country on the topic of legacy-wealth creation. It ignites my internal fire to spread the message of our history, legacy, and pursuits in ways that encourage everyone to consider joining the journey along the NarrowRoad to legacy wealth.

One day I was presenting to a group of extremely high-net-worth individuals who shared the same hesitation of talking about money with their friends and family as people without money often do.

One woman said, "I can't talk about money with my kids; they might share it with their friends in school."

I said, "Imagine that. Fifth graders talking about money ... these kids might learn early how well a banker does for a living and the methods in which Mommy and Daddy are using to chart a path for their financial future." Hmmm ... I wondered out loud, "If the wealth conversation started by fifth grade, by tenth grade financial perspectives of what things are worth would be different. By college, a budget would be their friend, and by graduation from college an investment group would be the way to remain in touch. Imagine that."

Nothing happens until something moves. It's time to un-mute our voices about money, wealth, and everything in between. That requires us to be vulnerable with others about what matters most. It's scary at first but soon you will find it opens a window of opportunity you never knew existed. In my sessions across the country when people open up about their relationship with money things shift, opening up the opportunity for relationships to build at a standard not possible in the storm. When in the storm your individual capacity is all you have to work with. Getting out of the storm is building a team to begin a more strategic relationship with money. This allows you to carry a path towards the wealth outcomes you desire and want to believe in.

The first step along the NarrowRoad is vision, second is thought, third is action, fourth step is speech, and the last step along the NarrowRoad is to anchor your journey to a series of desired outcomes. It's great to look long term, dream big, work hard, and exchange with people who have shared interests. Without measured goals and objectives, you can lose sight of the necessary connections between your past and present goals and your future financial and life expectations. We need to anchor the bends in your road so that you remember to continually shift your perspective from income to the necessary steps of wealth creation. As you will soon learn there are different degrees of freedom (income, class, independence, and investment), which require different types of relationships with the capital you have at your disposal. As you grow you become better equipped to manage the relationships required to build, grow, and expand our legacy wealth perspective. When in the storm it is all up to what you can do with the time you have and the talents you can afford to work with. At first being in the storm gives a person a sense of power, you are unstoppable, it is all up to you. While great at first, it s not sustainable long term. In the storm you believe the ability to keep it moving is progress when it is really going no where fast. Getting out of the storm, a topic we will discuss in chapter 13 is easier than you think once equipped with your NarrowRoad Identity.

The storm is why some of our elders resist writing wills—because they don't want the family to fight over their money and property upon their death. As a result, their legacy creates an additional job—buying one's parents' and grandparents' legacy assets out of probate once they transition. Without anchors to remind us to shift our perspective, we often avoid what appears to be uncharted territory, when instead it is one circle of legacy—the way forward is back through. Getting out of the storm is picking up the torch that has been left for you, adding your flame to it, and shining light in the dark places you see value in pursuing. It is also about taking the time to talk about what financially matters most to you and igniting the flames of others to join your journey, so the chain of legacy wealth remains unbroken and expands with those who can now see the road beyond what they know.

Looking through a Mirror Darkly

Throughout my journey it has been a constant occurrence that people, who on the surface seem to have it all together, will walk up to me and say, "I need to talk to you. I make too much money not to have none," or "If my family and friends really knew the financial reality I face, I would be in trouble." Grown men and women come to me saying, "If I go to my parents one more time for financial help, they will disown me." I interviewed countless people who used their inheritance to pay off debt only to return to same exact financial position of financial crisis a year later. Imagine, inheriting wealth that took a lifetime to build and using it to pay off short term debt. A lifetime of building, spent on a the culmination of a lifestyle of spending. It happens every day. This is how legacy wealth can be lost in one generation. The fear of facing reality about our finances is what keeps us in the storm, but on the other side of the storm is an elevated way of stewarding, a better way to manage what matters most to you with a more authentic relationship with money. What it really takes to elevate money to wealth is commitment to getting past survival, and establishing a healthy relationship with money that can pass on for generations.

It takes three generations to build legacy wealth and only one generation to lose it. Everyone begins their financial journey with a choice to go it alone, to drop the torch and disconnect from the journey that started before you and remain in the storm. Along the NarrowRoad to legacy wealth you are not alone. Three generations of friends and family, bankers, and financial instruments keep the wealth building, growing, and expanding. Are you alone in your financial journey? It's time to plan a way out of the storm. Survival is but a dimension of your life journey. Everyone, regardless of financial position, begins in the storm along the NarrowRoad. The promise of legacy wealth is progress; each generation will do better than the generation before them. It's time to connect the dots to order your steps to build a system to elevate your standard of legacy to wealth creation.

Weathering the Storm

The following are questions to help you better understand the NarrowRoad you're traveling. Answer as honestly as you can (if you're honest with yourself, your road will narrow to a path conducive to your success). There are no right or wrong answers, even if they don't match everything you've read in this book—remember, for legacy wealth to be attainable, it must be defined by you and the choices you understand.

Describe life experiences, positive and negative, that have helped you prepare for this long term financial journey (e.g., a healthy 401k or 403b, bankruptcy, a large savings account, a financially irresponsible partner):

What do you least understand about personal finance?

What was your relationship with money growing up?

Has that relationship changed any?

What elements of your financial life do you most need help with?

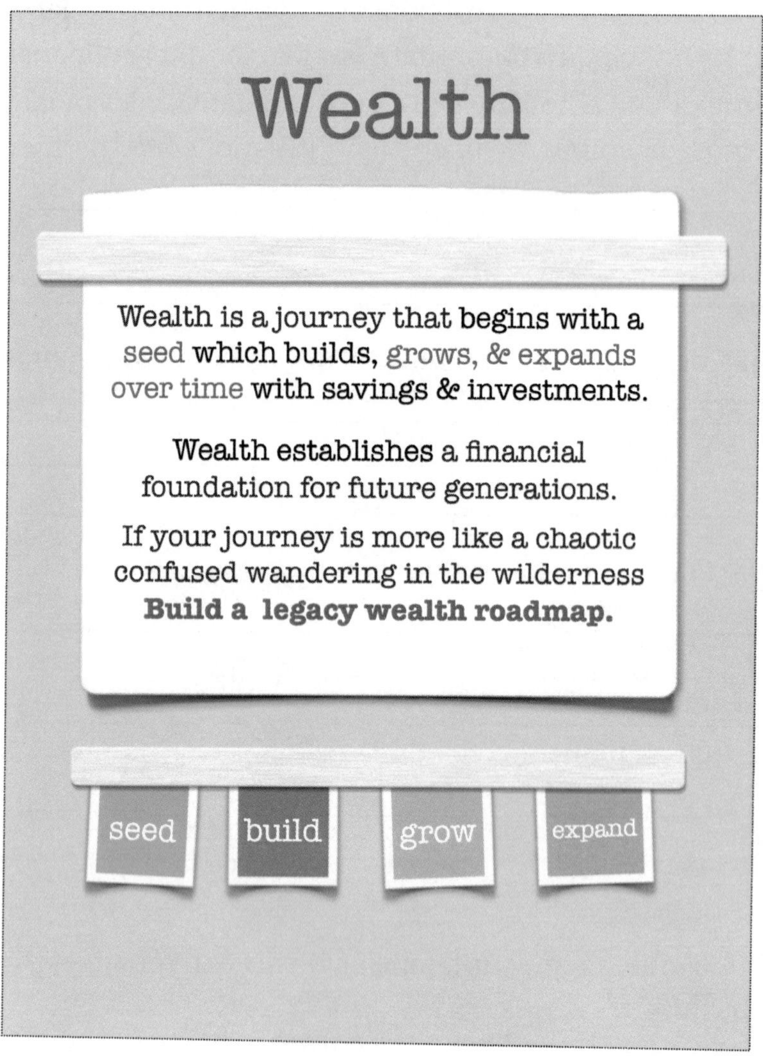

Mynarrowroad.com/wealth

Chapter 5: How Do You Build Wealth?

There is an African proverb: "If you want to go fast, go alone; if you want to far, go together." For wealth to pass across generations, it must be a group process—it takes a collective group of people, strategies, financial instruments, and plans to build wealth your way. It also takes an understanding of history, its patterns, and the opportunity the patterns of history create.

Building wealth our way is a way we culturally understand. We know this. Yet most of us are doing everything ourselves—we are personally taking on the full burden of earning income, spending it, trying to save, trying to invest, trying to own something of value, and pass that value on to the next generation, with the hopes that they will do the same. Anyone trying to do all these things alone is in what I call the storm. The storm is when you carry the load of everything. Essentially you have six jobs and are only getting paid for the one you have developed the most talent to build income with.

The last ten years of my Jolly-journey have given me extreme insight into the various types of relationships with money that exist in our communities and households. I gained most of my insight from the data I collected during a national assessment of faith and finance I conducted in support of the creation of the NarrowRoad and my doctoral research. I talked to more than sixty-eight hundred people about their relationship with money, ownership, business, and desires for legacy wealth. I studied the patterns and created a series of algorithms to lead others beyond the financial wilderness and onto a road toward wealth creation. I tested my findings with thousands people in seminars, lectures, classes, and church groups, among others, and have been sharing my understanding of the importance of legacy wealth across the country ever since.

Along the journey, so many people would respond in disbelief to my question, "Do you share your financial goals with those you love?"

They often say, "Share my financial goals and objectives with friends and family? What! I could never do that!"

Why not? I ask them.

Responses include:

I am a private person!

I don't like talking about money!

They might share my plan with others!

Nobody sees things the way I do about money!

I just feel uncomfortable doing that!

To that I say ... hmmm. My research and studies have shown that without trust in a relationship, there can be little to no meaningful exchange. The biggest obstacle to working together in community is often thought to be trust. Groups with the best intentions often hit roadblocks when it comes to trusting one another with key things like money, responsibility to plan things, the ability to execute, or the capacity to deliver. These choices leave us in the storm of doing everything ourselves.

Wealth is not created in isolation. Wealth has a language all its own with definitions that are shared, trusted, and of course understood. To get there, you must develop a comfort level talking about money, wealth, ownership, and legacy. This is a conversation that expands beyond the hope-and-dream state. This is not a brainstorming of what could be, this is a sharing of what will be. That is where wealth begins.

What I found in my research is that lack of trust is a symptom of something deeper—a lack of organization. In many cases, we are not structured in our financial matters, which leads to a misunderstanding of what is valuable independently and what is more valuable when shared. I for one was raised with the belief that you can't lose something God gave you, yet we are tight-lipped when it comes to wealth and legacy. As a result, our elders can tell us what to do but not how to do it. Which often leaves us wandering in the storm in the financial wilderness during the prime years of our window of opportunity to build wealth.

Mutual funds, the stock market, living trusts, and wills all require groups to plan and execute.

The storm that lives in the financial wilderness is why some inherit property and resources and then spend years afraid to touch it because they don't know how to discuss with their siblings what to do with it. The storm is why some work hard all their lives and have little to show for it when it comes to retirement.

Yet the simple principles of time, value of money, and compound interest reveal that the sooner we engage our window of opportunity with a legacy perspective, the more time we have to build the savings we need to grow the wealth we most desire. With structure we become organized, and with organization we become clearer about what needs to be shared to multiply.

What I also found was that the lack of organization around our possessions and experiences that we valued when commingled with society's definition of what is important led us to hold on to everything, fearing the risk of losing anything. What we lacked was a roadmap, a system to navigate both the risk and return of exchanging things of value for what is most valuable to our desired standard of living.

The #1 Thing You Need to Build Wealth

Your NarrowRoad ID reveals many things including the key element in required for your wealth building process. Everyone along the NarrowRoad has a weakness that needs structure, something they struggle with when trying to do alone. Systems are key to building wealth your way. Consider the role in your fourth quadrant a your perceived weakness that when supported by others becomes your most innate strength. It is the root of your purpose, located in your fourth quadrant. Want a key to building wealth your way? Ask for support with either your vision process, thought process, action process, or emotional process and watch how the impossible becomes possible to build wealth your way. See the below chart to determine which key is yours to get past what blocks you.

Wealth Needs		☑
Models	A model that aligns with your vision of wealth and shows a clear path to get there	☐
Strategies	A proven method or process that educates and helps you facilitate key wealth decisions	☐
Structure	A tactical, practical system that advises you and holds you accountable	☐
Engagement	A group to share and pursue ideas and plans with	☐

Who Is Part of Your Wealth Group?

Think of the wealth group process as a value chain, where each link is integral to getting further down the road toward your desired destination. The first link of value is your vision, however far down the road you are willing to consider. Taking the time to reflect on your past, present and desired future is what is first needed to build a wealth group process. There is a statistic that your net worth is often the average of your five closest friends. Think about your core group of friends. Is it true? When I shared this concept of the group process, many people who saw wealth as an important outcome to reach shared with me the question, "But what about my childhood friends who did not choose the paths I chose?"

It's a valid question, and one that keeps many families and friends stuck in the avoidance zone of relationships. I have a dear friend who, when she and her husband chose to place their daughter in private school, decided to assist the parents of their daughter's best friend so she could have her close friend with her. Their daughter's friend's parents had good jobs but had a different outlook on finances. I asked my friend if she and her husband ever considered talking about wealth choices they had made to prepare for their children's future and retirement. They had invested early in property and put money aside for both children's college education, they lived comfortably by looking at their household as a business with various streams of income, and they shared investments across generations and groups of friends. They had their group process yet were still anxious about having the conversation with someone who could use the straightforward conversation and tangible proof of what is possible.

Your wealth group must include the professionals—legal tax, and financial. It must also include family across generations—parents, grandparents, cousins, nieces, nephews. It further expands when you can include friends. The legacy expands and continues beyond those with the degrees, access, and know-how to those with ideas, dreams, and a will to do if only there was an invitation to join a group focused on defining wealth their way and achieving it.

Wealth is a group process—never forget it.

Part 3: Our Pursuit

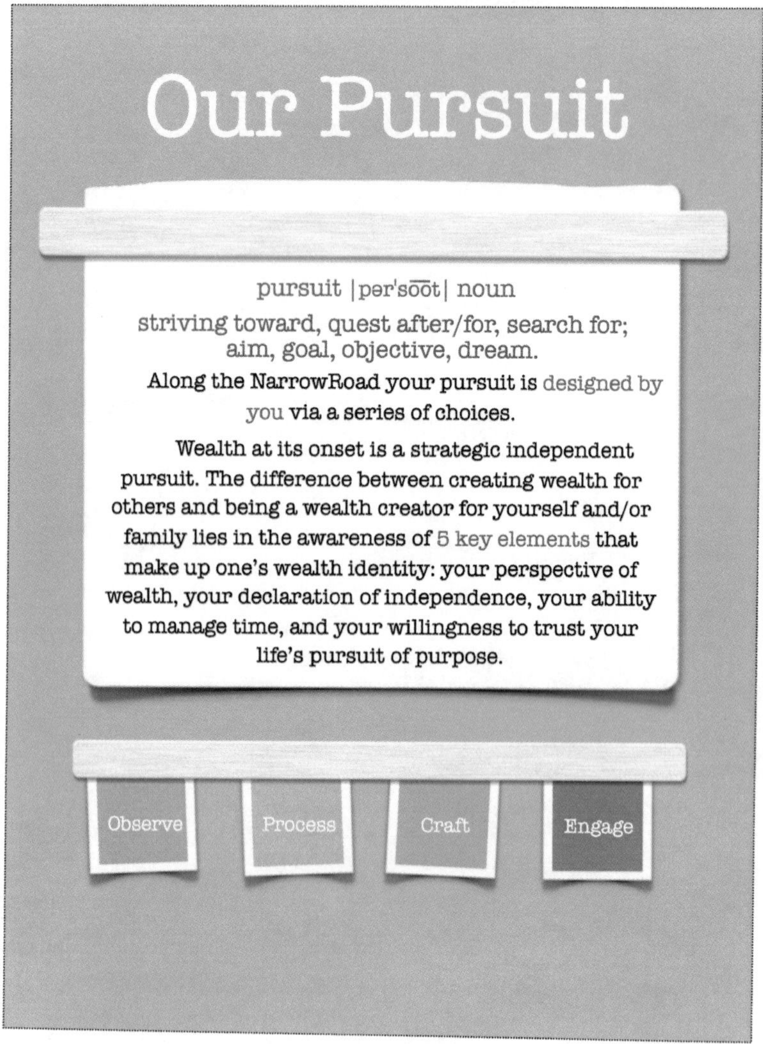

Mynarrowroad.com/pursuit

A pursuit is the action of following or pursuing someone or something. In our case, our pursuit is navigating beyond the generations that came before us.

Our Pursuit Answers the Question: Where Do We Go from Here?

This question is borrowed from one of the prophetic legacy narratives that set the wisdom of the NarrowRoad—Dr. Martin Luther King Jr. Dr. King was wise enough to not leave this question open. He narrowed it with two choices, chaos or community. Along the NarrowRoad your pursuit is designed by you. It is a series of choices:

- ☐ Lifestyle or legacy
- ☐ Chaos or community
- ☐ Fast or far
- ☐ Surface or deep
- ☐ Baby step or quantum leap

Throughout my research journey I uncovered three roadblocks common in just about everyone's pursuit. At the end of each interview I would share my ultimate desired outcome for the NarrowRoad, which is legacy wealth. The responses would initially always come back the same—"That will never happen," "We won't work together," "No one is going to be open and honest about their money," or "Wealth is not for everybody."

Year after year of hearing these patterned responses revealed that there are three primary issues blocking our pursuit of wealth:

- ❑ Trust
- ❑ Access to capital
- ❑ Leadership

Here are the real roadblocks that lie beneath the surface of our primary issues.

- ❑ Lack of organization
- ❑ Lack of acumen
- ❑ Lack of purpose

What is in the way of your pursuit? Is it an inability to trust others with your innermost hopes and dreams? Or is it a lack of capital to fund what you want in life and legacy? Perhaps it is a need for a model to show the way. What lies underneath that roadblock is the design for your pursuit. Your NarrowRoad identity (NRID) is the key that unlocks these obstacles in your life so that you can pursue the opportunities that live in your answer to Dr. King's question, where do you go from here? What is it you can't see clearly?

The road to wealth is narrow. Few find the path to fund it in time to enjoy it. Finding it early is ideal but finding it is critical to navigate out of the financial wilderness. Part two of this book is focused on legacy, specifically your legacy narrative. Right now you might have a story that details your family journey to date but do you have a narrative? A narrative along the NarrowRoad is different from a story. We all have stories. Stories follow the loop of a beginning a middle and an end. Legacy narratives never end they shine light on the direction forward extending the invitation to the inheritor of the legacy to carry the story forward. As such, it is important to know your story and connect it to the stories that came before you with a narrative of the forward movement of the business of life called you.

The old folks say the way forward is back through (that's wisdom, by the way). The mission of this section of the book is to focus you on your legacy so that you can unearth the talents required for a successful pursuit of wealth however you will soon come to define it.

Chapter 6: Steps along The NarrowRoad

Along the NarrowRoad are steps that create a personal business system for success. A business is a series of valued exchanges that when connected form a chain that builds in scale over time. The larger the desired outcome the larger the business system. Owning your steps along the NarrowRoad is how the system becomes custom tailored to you. The steps along the NarrowRoad once connected form an equation capable of keeping you on your very own road for success. Equations contain a promise that when you apply mathematical relationships to a set of variables you will arrive at an expected outcome. Equations can also help you solve for the unknown. Consider your NRID as the key that unlocks the equation for your success.

Everyone begins the NarrowRoad in a storm; where you are in some way doing things on your own that are best pursued with others. Getting out of the storm begins with a shift in perspective. To shift your perspective, each NarrowRoad journey begins with the questions what wealth is to you and what do you need to learn to feel more confident in your plan to build it?

The NarrowRoad system links vital elements of your life in a custom way unique to your wealth identity. Your wealth identity is called the NarrowRoad ID (NRID). We uncovered your NRID as part of your assignment in chapter 1. This is the key to unlocking your wealth codes along the road that narrows and shifts with the indicators unique to you.

Our history plays an important part in seeding one's pursuit of life purpose, which can lead to legacy wealth. As benefactors of history, we have a unique shared narrative from which to pull from.

Each NarrowRoad journey begins by separating the key elements of your picture into a framework that brings clarity. Your unique way of visioning, thinking, doing, and speaking will become the foundation of your journey. Once you learn your system for success via the base equation, you have a deeper clarity that will ultimately lead to a dimension of freedom few find and even fewer pursue.

Understanding the history that came before you, specifically the decisions that led to where we are today in society plays an important role in framing our picture we are posing for together. This macro view frames the picture we are all posing for inviting the individual to fully participate in the collective group process we are all navigating together.

To appreciate and value the wealth identity revealed in your NRID, you must take the steps along the NarrowRoad to understand and own its parts. The NarrowRoad is based on this premise. Lets explore the elements that make up every legacy-wealth building equation so the NarrowRoad can work for you.

The NarrowRoad principles are

1. Vision: seeing is believing
2. Thought: belief drives action
3. Action: action reveals purpose
4. Speech: purpose speaks your truth
5. Outcomes: truth delivers promises

Seeing is believing

How far down the road are you looking?

NarrowRoad Step #1—Vision

Step One is seeing is believing. This step focuses on clarifying how far down the road you are presently looking. There is a dimension of vision that invites you to invest the time to understand what came before you. The elders have a saying: "The way forward is back through." This investment in hindsight helps clarify the areas along your road that are vulnerable to blind spots. It is from this perspective the NarrowRoad explores the depth of vision required to solve for unknowns in its base equation. Beginning with an initial legacy narrative, each journeyer navigates a metapattern of the previous three generations of history to obtain clarity of perspective about their personal answer to the question, "Where do we go from here?" A metapattern is a pattern of patterns, and the NarrowRoad metapattern is the patterns found in the stages of financial and business acumen, our American history, your theology, and risk inherent in everyone's journey to pursue what you most desire. You have to see how it impacts you to believe it.

How Far down the Road Are You Looking—Lifestyle or Legacy?

The beauty of a vision is that it comes in stages, like glimpses of light in just the right places made available and evident to you. Vision emerges in the places where your knowledge grows dim or the opportunity seems to be beyond the scope of your experiences. Glimpses are those chance moments where you see parts of a whole that have not completely come into plain view. For some, this type of sight is more of a knowing than an actual vision, something almost intuitive. Throughout my journey, I have often run into people who say things like, "I just know I am not supposed to end my life in such a negative financial state," or "This has to stop with me; my children must have a different experience with the financial realities of life."

My observations revealed the various financial challenges we face throughout our lives happen at inflection points that are often recognizable to older generations yet seldom discussed before the next generation can do anything to avoid it. And so the pattern continues in yet another leg of our history. Some of these challenges stem from early childhood experiences, some from poor choices made in early adulthood, and some are the result of a poorly planned retirement. Financial challenges are prevalent, and our vision often becomes clear in the midst of crisis. These inflection points if we let them, strengthen our faith. They also if we let them narrow our road and clarify our vision on what is required to get out of wandering pattern within the financial wilderness.

While these experiences are shared by many; how we respond to these glimpses of light is something entirely different. Some simply choose to avoid them and run the other way when reminders of what they saw appear. It's an effort to keep the peace of ignorant bliss. Others dive deep into the fray, getting lost in the dark places imagining what they saw was more than it was, and others stand still and wait for the glimpse to reappear and invite themselves to peer closer and learn how to believe that yes, the time is now, that yes, this is change we can believe in, and yes, I can now afford to have the audacity to hope. The first principle of the NarrowRoad when applied to your unique NRID reveals the source of your unique ability to see what others cannot yet see. It helps better understand the depth of your perception and ways to clarify your next step beyond the present rocks in your road.

What is your #1 Role?________________________________

NarrowRoad™ Visionary Types		
Quadrant #1	**Your #1 Quadrant,** is how you **first SEE** the world. **Note:** Your **perspective** is your inherited equity, it is the unique lens that shows the way past obstacles and problems. You invest this equity when you share the way you see things everyday.	☑
Pure Visionary	Sees through the lens of wisdom: Your vision is long term, and culturally influenced. You have the wisdom but often not the resources to do all you see.	☐
Thinker - Visionary	Sees through the lens of knowledge: Your vision is near term and relies heavily on an internal need for proof. You need to see it first to believe it.	☐
Doer - Visionary	Sees through the lens of experience: Vision for the future is immediate and sparked by activity. You clarity comes from hands on activity.	☐
Speaker - Visionary	Sees through the lens of expression: Vision for the future is ongoing and sparked by engagement, connection, and feeling.	☐

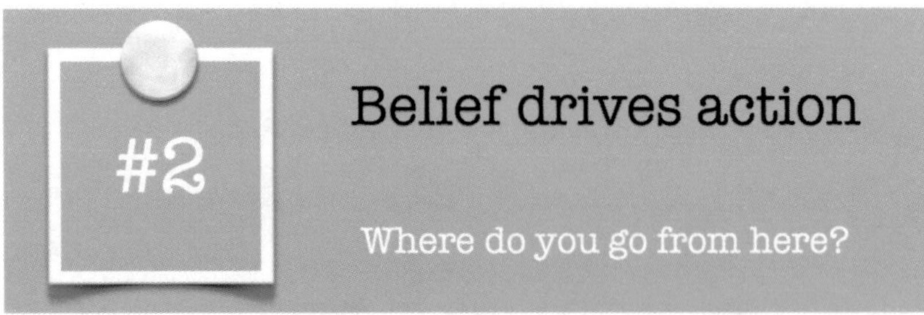

NarrowRoad Principle #2—Thought

Principle two, thought, focuses on declaring your independence. Wealth at its onset is a strategic independent pursuit. It is for this reason that the second principle of the NarrowRoad is concentrated around thought.

Thought is the key to independence. If you can believe it, you will find your own way of confidently doing it. In other words, belief drives action, and a belief system is really a strategy to navigate beyond the pitfalls everyone faces when in pursuit of a promise.

Your belief system supports what you know to be true. Along my journey, I wanted to understand if there was in fact this Promised Land that both the Bible and history speak of, then why haven't we gotten there yet? Why did it feel like we are still wandering around the wilderness? What I found was, there is a pattern to the wilderness, and within it are hidden elements that one can get trapped in easily without a clear strategy. There is a wilderness of distance between an idea of a promise and taking possession of a Promised Land. Navigating this distance leaves a lot to journey through that is largely unseen to the naked eye and untrained mind.

Wealth is a journey of a series of decisions that build, grow, and expand over time with savings and investments—we all know this. So why can some people pass wealth from generation to generation while others seem to remain stuck in the income lane?

This is the question I asked of the elders in my study because they had lived to see a lot of wandering in the wilderness. I wanted to get their glimpses of the dark places that seem to generationally elude us.

One woman said, "There is no roadmap for the systems that operate around one's life work. Most folks just know how to work with what is in front of them. Pamela, if you want more people to build wealth? Well, you're going to have to draw a map for them to see it and then teach them how to believe it." She herself had built wealth in her lifetime, owning several homes and land that went as far back as her great-grandfather, but it would not pass, unfortunately, because both of her sons, while college educated, lived in her house and could not find work. She feared the way her sons were spending their inheritance while she was alive that her wealth would sustain their lifetime but nothing more. Neither of her sons were married, had no children, no one would live to see what she had worked so hard to build but them.

Wealth systems are different from work systems. Wealth creators have unblinded faith that their investments will reap a harvest over time. They invest in the unseen promises of what is to come and have become accustomed to looking for hidden treasure. Income creators often have blind faith about the harvest that will come after the work has been completed. Work, even social life, is a constant stream of decisions. The common element in these decisions is that they are not made in isolation. You are surrounded in a wilderness by other journeyers whose choices intersect with yours. These interactions at times seem random on an individual level, and when looked at from afar demonstrate patterns, patterns that fund systems that build wealth each and every day.

What I found on my journey was that wealth creators have a financial strategy for their lives that becomes tradition and passes from generation to generation. Wealth creators have learned to value intangible currencies that lead to access to build even more wealth, with additional capitals such as cultural, intellectual, and social. This financial strategy forms a collective level of expertise that has been acquired from the trials and errors of generations before them all in pursuit of a purpose. Over time, the day-to-day management of this wealth-creating strategy is outsourced to people and institutions with even more expertise, and the pattern of wealth becomes a system that continues.

Those who are skillful creators of wealth for others have a work strategy for their life that fluctuates with each work situation or job. The difference between creating wealth for others and being a wealth creator for yourself and/or family lies in the awareness of key elements that make up one's wealth identity: your perspective of wealth, your declaration of independence, your ability to manage time, and your willingness to trust your life's pursuit of purpose. It is not all up to you, wealth creation is a convergence of people, places, and things all working together for the good of a promise whose time has come with you.

Most of these are things you often cannot yet see. As I have said before, wealth is not just money, an example of a wealth system that does not directly include money is an individuals health system. When one views health as wealth, he or she has a strategy to maintain good health, which includes good insurance, regular checkups, and building relationships with doctors you trust. It's taking care of the body that will be the vehicle you will need to pass on wealth to the next generation.

My father, for instance, had two bouts with cancer (June 2013 and May 2014). If not for his history with his chosen set of physicians, he would have not survived the first bout. Daddy went into remission late November 2013. His cancer returned with a vengeance the following May. It was his trust in his doctors and our trust in God that made a painful, difficult season bearable. The love demonstrated by the doctors and nurses who had grown accustomed to caring for my father was made possible by the time my father invested with them while he was healthy.

My father passed away in late June 2014 in the company of friends and family, which included his team of physicians. By investing the time to preserve his health via his relationship with doctors he could trust, they prescribed the best early treatment to extend the time we had with my father. Again, I repeat: there are wealth systems, and there are work systems—money is nothing but time spent. Death is a gift in the lessons it gives those left behind to ensure the legacy continues.

Along my journey, I have discovered that this awareness can be taught or at least encouraged, which gives people a better chance to strategize how best to incorporate wealth systems into their work systems. Maximizing the wealth potential of your income is the way to include the present and the future in your strategy to get out of the wilderness. This becomes what

I call your strategic advantage that can be passed on for generations. The Second step when applied to your NRID reveals how you best process information to create a strategy for financial independence you believe in.

What is your #2 Role? ____________________

NarrowRoad™ Thinker Types		
Quadrant #2	**Your #2 Quadrant** how you **THINK.** **Note:** Your second role is the way you process information, grow, evaluate ideas and build confidence. This is the key that unlocks your genius code as you pursue independence.	☑
Visionary - Thinker	Thought process is based on independent observations. You often need to take a step back and see the bigger picture to increase confidence.	☐
Pure Thinker	Thought process is based on learning and thinking things through independently. You often requires additional time alone to reach a a level of confidence about an opportunity.	☐
Doer - Thinker	Thought process is based on independent activity. You often figure things out by spending time doing it on your own and or "working it through with your hands."	☐
Speaker - Thinker	Thought process is based on engagement and inquiry. You often can translate what others are thinking into a language most can understand.	☐

Action reveals purpose

Is your doing creating a difference?

NarrowRoad Principle #3—Action

The third step of the NarrowRoad is action. Action is absolutely essential to your pursuit of legacy wealth. Consistent doing makes the difference between a dream of wealth and a mission to create it. The initial exodus deposited the Israelites into the wilderness on the way to the Promised Land. There were specific things they had to do to take full possession of it. In the wilderness each member of each tribe had a job to do, the tribes operated under one of four standards. When the silver trumpet blew everyone knew what his or her mission was to move further down the road to another part of the wilderness.

How much wealth is "enough"? Have you taken the time to calculate a personal level of enough? Enough what, you ask? Enough resources to build wealth your way. Wealth creation is really up to you and how you define it. Along the NarrowRoad you will learn that if everyone can create wealth for others, they can surely create wealth for themselves. It's all in the way you value your talents and abilities. Your time is extremely important in your calculation of enough. For some in the Promised Land narrative, wandering in the wilderness was "enough", for others it was going further down the road and taking possession of an inherited promise. What is enough for you?

Your life is a portfolio of assets. Your journey occurs during a timed window of opportunity. Capacity, commitment, and persistence are necessary elements of a fruitful journey with various harvests. However, they are not what will get you to the position of enough. Some people work their whole lives toward the expected harvest of retirement, only to find they do not have the capacity or the resources to enjoy life as they had hoped. Your thought pattern formed in the wilderness raises the awareness of what is needed to create an action pattern. Your action pattern is the way you do things to create the resources needed for enough and beyond. The NarrowRoad principle for action is "action reveals purpose." What do you do best? It is our personal human capital that we will use to build our life portfolio, it is our blood, sweat, and tears that creates the life we desire to live. This translates into developing your talents that create the lifestyle business of you — a specific way you choose to multiply your talents to create the life you need and if you desire to get past "enough", the life you really want. Belief drives action, action drives creativity, creativity ignites income creation, and income creation drives wealth creation.

Throughout my research, I have found that whatever you believe you can do is exactly what you can do. We've all heard the old adage that time is money. Well, time is not just money, it really is so much more. Everything takes time to create—from a rewarding career to the fulfillment of a promise. The extent to which you believe in your abilities is not exclusive of what you are capable of, but it does carry the highest probability of what you will attempt. While this does enable one to have a variety of successful experiences, it leaves a lot of resources untapped and underdeveloped. These untapped and underdeveloped resources, with a little faith, could finance your pursuit of legacy wealth. The third principle when applied to your unique NRID reveals the talent most useful for your income earning pursuit.

What is your #3 Role? ______________________

NarrowRoad™ Doer Types		
Quadrant #3	**Your #3 Quadrant** is your **PRIMARY ASSET** **Note:** Your third role the easiest element of your identity to MONETIZE and the key talent you are recognized for.	☑
Visionary - Doer	Your strength is driven by your ability to see the end goal and focus the efforts of others to attain it. You align the end with the beginning. With insight you develop moving parts into a model that works.	☐
Thinker - Doer	Your strength is driven by your ability to use your knowledge to identify improve the current situation. You consult with others to understand who desire to know how to improve. With the right information you make things better .	☐
Pure Doer	Your strength is driven by your ability to complete necessary steps to to create momentum. With the right to-do list you get things done.	☐
Speaker - Doer	Your strength is driven by your ability to intuit the needs of the current situation and speak in ways that motivate and encourage others. You words encourage, direct, and guide the way forward. With the right message you move mountains.	☐

Life & Death is in your tongue

Does your life speak your truth?

The NarrowRoad Principle #4—Speech

The fourth step along the NarrowRoad is speech. This principle is concentrated on the importance of finding your voice, and defining your message to build your definition of freedom in the Promised Land that will be owned by you. The Israelites escaped Egyptian slavery transitioning into a wilderness period that was not slavery, but also not yet entirely freedom by their own design. Within freedom resides an understanding that in order to stay there you must maintain a standard of life that you desire and are willing to work, save and invest to continue to afford to keep operating. To do this you must find your voice, to ask for what you want, and respond to the invitations that come to assist you in getting there.

Your voice expresses what you feel; it is the energy that keeps the promise alive and capable of transferring across generations. Your speech is what builds the energy required for a collective pursuit of a desired degree of freedom. Along the NarrowRoad speech is how you use your voice, it's what invites others to collaborate with you along your journey. It is in many ways why people connect with you. Yet many consciously or unconsciously remain silent, stuck between various stages of pursuit toward the Promised Land, waiting for the right time to speak our truth.

Why is this? Is it due to fear of rejection, fear of acceptance, or a lack of clarity defining the truth? Is it a need to define the key words that determine the level of wealth we desire to create? Words such as lifetime value, middle class, and legacy? How does one define freedom in ways that others will understand and perhaps want to subscribe to? What is democracy and how does your voice contribute to it? Becoming more conscious of our personal answers to these collective questions is how we unmute; it is how we find our voices and build a standard that supports our desired degree of freedom for our personal business, our immediate and extended family businesses, and our broader community business. Yet we all in our own way speak differently, our voices all don't sound the same, don't come from the same place. Owning your voice is a two-step process; along the NarrowRoad, step number four is about finding the origin of your voice.

The creation of the Constitution, the outcomes the Israelites faced in the final leg of the journey to the Promised Land, and the aftermath of the nightmare that followed Dr. King's dream that sought unity and justice for America are examples of the importance of building a life system that speaks your truth in ways that pass on for generations. How does on go about building a voice that speaks beyond the audible sound of the moment to leave a lasting message? Unmuting your voice breaks the pattern of repeated the mistakes of the past. While it is the second to the last step along the it is one of the most important.

Silence rears its head during our childhood. As kids we don't have the ability or the skills to sort through life's complicated events, so we end up burying those emotions and attaching a specific judgment to them. These events can be as simple as being laughed at during your first day of school or as detrimental as witnessing the death of a loved one. As kids, our ideas of the world and where we fit into it was still developing —yet when a defining moment arises, it marks on the worksheet of who we are in a painful way. This very unique pain—which is unique to each of us—it lies in the shadows of our being. Unable to sort through this childhood pain or disappointment forces us (as adults) to make decisions in order to avoid that same feeling or the memory of it. It's difficult to revisit that unique childhood in order to heal, but we must unpack that wound to release our voice.

If you are unhappy with our world today, my question to you is what truth is your life speaking? The fourth principle when applied to your unique NRID reveals just how you uniquely can start to unmute to secure the solutions you need.

What is your fourth role? ______________________

NarrowRoad™ Speaker Types		
Quadrant #4	**Your #4 Quadrant** is how you **SPEAK**, or send messages. Note: Your fourth role is your weakest and most undeveloped role in your inventory of treasure. This is the key that once matured will be your greatest source of strength and freedom	☑
Visionary - Speaker	You eyes tell the real story; you have the ability to see through words, and expressions of others when in a group. Your emotions often impact your ability to see clearly.	☐
Thinker - Speaker	You mind speaks your real truth; you can synthesize the opinions of others in a group. Your emotions often impact your ability to make decisions	☐
Doer - Speaker	You actions speak louder than your words, and you prefer group collaboration to get things done. Your emotions impact your ability to do things consistently.	☐
Pure Speaker	Your words speak the real truth; you have the ability to say what everyone else is really feeling. Your emotions impact how much you share and with who.	☐

Truth delivers outcomes

Is your best further down the road?

The NarrowRoad Principle #5—Outcome

The fifth step along the NarrowRoad is outcome—truth delivers on promises in the form of a definitive outcome. This principle is concentrated on the importance of anchoring your journey to a series of milestones and metrics that keep you focused on continuing to progress further down the road beyond survival, beyond freedom, to growth to expansion. The fifth step of the NarrowRoad supports the belief that legacy wealth is anchored to a multigenerational pursuit of a definable outcome that starts with a seed and builds and grows over time. Your first desired outcome will be based on elements from the prior four principles and influenced by those in your family line that journeyed ahead of you. These become a series of legacy metrics that are further defined by financial milestones. The ultimate desired outcomes to be achieved throughout your lifetime is the continued execution of your legacy wealth blueprint. A written vision that contains three defined milestones leading further down the road toward what is possible for you to achieve given your current situation.

I have found that the road to wealth is paved with good intentions—many dream of becoming and remaining wealth creators, many create the financial plan, some consult with a financial advisor, and or have an idea for how their life will financially play out. What is lacking is a method of accountability and consistency to keep those mentioned above who have the best intentions, focused the promise that lay ahead of them when they remain committed to their personal NarrowRoad principles for legacy wealth.

The blind spots along the road, such as the lack of accountability, lack of accepted methods of measurement, lack of follow through in personal financial performance, and lack of models of successful pursuits of legacy wealth; the elements of the how-to becomes a secret, something kept from the very people in your wealth group who need to hear, learn, see, and follow your lead to attain it. And the wandering continues.

This fifth step along the NarrowRoad enables everyone who desires to get to the promise of legacy wealth to create a way that holds themselves and those they love most accountable to a vision whose time has finally come. Desired outcomes show clearly what together you as a family or group can do in this lifetime and beyond. Desired outcomes can pass on for generations, they can be shared across friends and families. Your desired outcomes begin as something personal to you, and end as a glimpse of light in the dark places we all face while in the financial wilderness. Your desired outcome once achieved becomes a model others can study and follow if they choose to. This is how step number five expands the legacy wealth narrative in a language understood by you. Charting your path in this way becomes not just something worthwhile for you, but also for others who want to believe as you do but need that glimpse of light called you.

What is your desired outcome? ____________________

NarrowRoad™ Outcome Types		
Quadrant #5	**Your #5 Quadrant contains** the desired outcomes at the end of each bend in the NarrowRoad. **Note:** Your fifth quadrant is what shadows your progress along your journey. It becomes your anchor that does not change until you have attained your desired outcome.	☑
Legacy Outcome	**Long Term Outcome:** To pass on wealth to the next generation. (However you define it.)	☐
Growth Outcome	**Near Term:** To grow beyond living a lifestyle to the pursuit of financial independence by owning the business of you.	☐
Mission Outcome	**Immediate:** To Create a realistic budget, move beyond survival and consistently multiply your talents to attain a degree of freedom that satisfies your wants and needs.	☐
Purpose Outcome	**Ongoing:** To build and pursue a standard of wealth for myself and share the journey with others I care about.	☐

Your NarrowRoad™ Equation

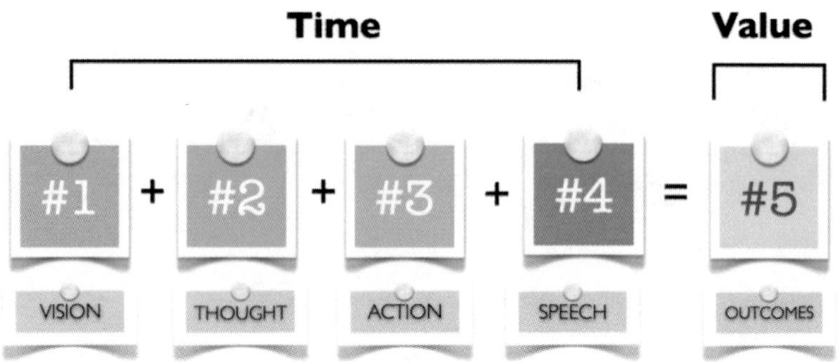

How you create, build, grow, and expand wealth along your NarrowRoad™ journey is unique to your NRID.
This is how you build wealth for yourself.

Key Elements of the NarrowRoad Equation

The following are questions to help you better understand the NarrowRoad you're traveling. Answer as honestly as you can (if you're honest with yourself, your road will narrow to a path conducive to your success). There are no right or wrong answers, even if they don't match everything you've read in this book—remember, for legacy wealth to be attainable, it must be defined by you and the choices you understand.

Principle 1: Describe your first role (how you see): I see with my (hands, eyes, mind, mouth)

____

____

____

Principle 2: Describe your second role (how you think): I think with my hands, eyes, mind, mouth)

____

____

____

Principle 3: Describe your third role (how you do): I best operate with my (hands, eyes, mind, mouth)

____

____

____

Principle 4: Describe your fourth role (how you speak): I communicate my truth with my (hands, eyes, mind, mouth)

____

____

____

Principle 5: Considering the options above, Describe a desired outcome you have concerning wealth you want to pursue in your lifetime:

____

____

____

Chapter 7: Capital along The NarrowRoad

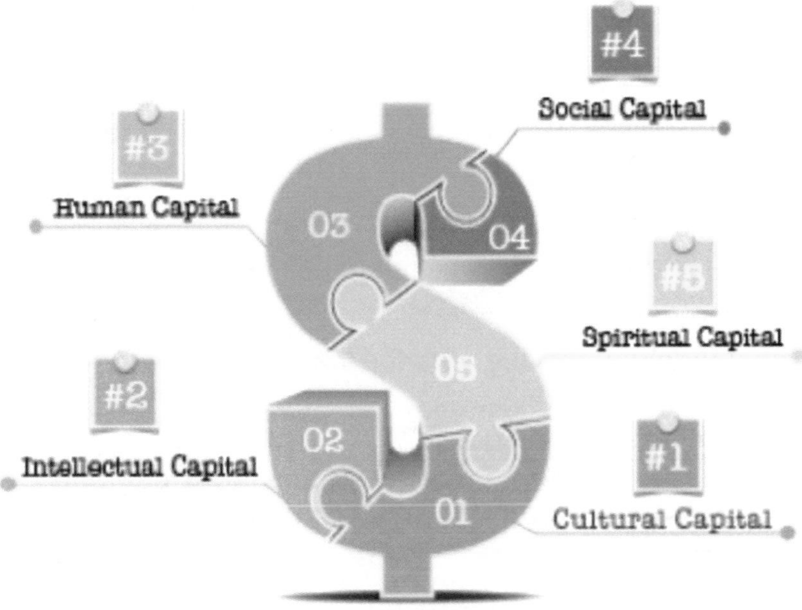

There are five forms of capital along the NarrowRoad —human, social, intellectual, cultural, and spiritual.

This capital makes up your portfolio of assets. Armed and confident of these five asset classes you have everything you need to fund your pursuit of the promise. In our society there is a belief we have a capital issue, that simply is not true, at best we have an allocation issue, at our worst we have a connection and a trust issue. With what you have been blessed with you can do what you are called to do. Our ancestors legacy narratives prove this.

To gain an understanding of this, let's talk about the business of you. The business of you uses capital to build, grow, and expand. The business of you is largely the same as everyone else's it has a product, a market, an opportunity cost and a price. Each of us in business has sixty minutes in an hour, twenty-four hours a day, and seven days a week. Everyone with a financial statement is in business. What is different between your business and any other's is your perspective and how your unique view influences the way you operate.

An operating model can be a complex system that determines what a business does, how it should do it, why it should do it, and who is in control of making sure it gets done.

A business remains in business by creating and selling a product. How do you make money? What is your product or talent multiplier? How do you deliver it? Why is it valuable? Whom determines the value? What capital do you use to create your product? Everyone in business must answer the what, how, why, and who questions about their operating model. Again, anyone with a financial statement is in business; anyone. Those who took the time and spent the money to incorporate are entrepreneurs, and those who work for someone else every day are intrapreneurs. The business is largely the same, it's just the perspectives that are different. To be clear, every one of us is in business to some extent.

Once Moses died, what I believe sparked the change in the wilderness wandering plan was the desire to be something more than a people who escaped Egyptian slavery and had break-even albeit blessed provisions. They desired to create and build something of their own. That decision required two things: the courage to fight for what is yours, and the determination to operate in your part of the promise with the old corn of the land (see Joshua 5:11). Essentially use what you have to get what you want and believe. Pure and simple.

The need to be able to answer operating questions about your business is more urgent than ever. Increasing pressure to earn more income for survival needs such as education and health care is real. We are living in a time when, operationally, many people are realizing that relying solely on the abilities you believe in most will, at best, supply only your base operating needs. This leads many to eliminate savings and investing from the operating plan in order to sustain the lifestyle they are used to.

This brings us back to the different degrees of freedom (income, class, independence, and investment) that were previously mentioned. How much can you do with the income generated from your efforts? Will it sustain you? If so, for how long? Answers to these questions reveal your degree of freedom. Want to move to the next degree of freedom? Elevate your standard of operating your business. How do you do that? Deepen your understanding of the best ways to allocate your portfolio of assets, the five capitals—cultural, intellectual, human, social, and spiritual.

One resource you can evaluate immediately is how you steward your time. Are you spending as much time creating wealth for yourself as you are for others (for example, through your job)? If belief drives action, what does this say about your operating belief system? If action reveals purpose, what are your financial actions revealing about you? Along the NarrowRoad these simple questions reveal the complex decisions that you are consciously and often unconsciously making while operating the business of you.

Why Five Capitals?

My journey revealed that there is a distinct connection between one's faith and finance. We all anchor our belief in something when considering success along our journeys. For some it is their own physical abilities or human capital ("I am going to work to make this happen"); for others it is their intellect or intellectual capital ("I know I will figure it out"); for others it is through the leveraging of their relationships or social capital ("I am going to call the right person to work this out in my favor"); and for others it is relying on their cultural awareness or cultural capital ("How did Grandmother handle this?"). Yet in addition to those belief systems there was an additional one—belief in something outside yourself. Yes, along my journey I have come across atheists, agnostics, and believers, and please remember that my role along the NarrowRoad is that of facilitator, focused on guiding others along the principles and steps that lead to wealth their way. Part of how I do this is as a theologian. In this capacity, the NarrowRoad and I as the creator seek not to tell you what to believe; rather, the objective is to help you define what you believe about unseen opportunities that have yet to appear and the financing of them with all the capital within you.

The NarrowRoad is unique in that it seeks to reveal five critical components of your identity rather than the usual four found in personality and scientific typing tools such as Myers-Briggs and DNA to name a couple. For each aspect of your identity there is a capital associated with it. Along long the narrow road there are five steps each associated with a specific capital. Each step represents a quadrant, with four primary steps/ quadrants situated in a 2x2 matrix. The fifth capital, step or quadrant is similar to the fifth dimension it hovers over the primary four as that one additional step, that leap of faith that that sits squarely in the middle of who you are.

Each variable in your identity carries with it a capital that us used as a currency to fund your pursuit further down the road toward wealth as defined by you. I initially attempted to distill money and our relationship with it into categories of sociology(Q1), psychology (Q2), economics(Q3), and general systems theory (Q4). However, as I journeyed to make sense of the elements of capital as it relates to the fundamentals of society, in ways that formed currencies we trade every day there were some exchanges that did not fit neatly into a four-quadrant box.

I thought the NarrowRoad method could be understood as cultural, intellectual, human, and social capital that evolved into systems and structures that corporately exchanged data, information, insight, and value. This would provide a means for developing a basis for anyone to chart a path from their current financial situation to where ever they decided to go. All it would take was a series of investments and savings strategies to make the required exchanges. Much of this proved true. But there was this additional element, a currency that was not as transparent but readily available and expended by all I interviewed. Something invisible, immaterial and very real. The NarrowRoad as a result extended its reach to include a fifth quadrant or element; spiritual capital or faith. Since what I found was that whenever most grew uncertain about how to proceed or where to pursue something financially they just closed their eyes and believed.

The NarrowRoad thus argues that there are above ground (doing and speaking) and below ground realities (seeing and thinking) to any and everyone's relationship with money and wealth. Above ground there is a very impersonal reality about money, how you make it and how you spend it. Below ground there is more of an intangible and very transferable aspect about how you view money and wealth what you believe you and your relationship with money can do to build wealth.

The bridge between above and below is the fifth quadrant or element. It often connects the seen with the unseen and lends enlightenment, unity, order, and opportunity for independence in your relationship with money.

As a result, theology (Q5) became an integrative element in the NarrowRoad method. The preface of one of my favorite books, Heart to Head, written by second-generation black theologian Dwight Hopkins, "Sought to clarify the relation between faith and the struggle for social justice." In the book, Michael Dyson, a noted biblical scholar from Princeton, wrote the foreword and eloquently linked spirituality, religion, and theology in a frame I have come to live by. To borrow from his framework: "If spirituality is what they feel about transcendence, and religion is what we do about God, then theology is what we think about, what we feel and believe."

Keep this in mind as we explore the five capitals.

#1—Cultural Capital

Cultural capital along the NarrowRoad is the source of your wisdom. Consider it equity that makes your perspective unique to your inherited legacy narrative and capable of shining light onto others without your distinct point of view. Many of us discount the value of our equity perspective, reducing the lived histories of our family to show and tell versus invest and expand. Within the American narrative we share a unique history that changed drastically with Emancipation. What can you see because of it that others cannot? How does the wisdom gleaned from the migration strategy your family pursued influence your worldview? Remember seeing is believing for most, what viewpoint are or aren't you including in the road that lies in front of you?

When I first launched my company I began a journey to try some audacious things. Many of the people who I shared my dreams with thought it impossible, yet inside I was led to not let is dissuade me. When I shared my original vision for Torch with my grandmother Mildred Jolly, she shared with me the disappointments her father and father's father experienced. She told me that because of these failed attempts, she was confident success was in store for me. In one sharing, she shifted my perspective from crazy to carrying out the next degree of freedom for my family legacy.

What hidden equity lies in your portfolio of cultural capital? Perhaps this is what is required to fully execute the vision for the business of you.

#2—Intellectual Capital

Intellectual capital along the NarrowRoad not surprisingly begins with knowledge but it does not end there. This asset in your portfolio may not matter to much until you apply it. The value of your intellectual capital grows with applied knowledge, which means you have to use it. Education today is becoming increasingly expensive, the expectation that you are to apply what you learn to grow independent of the heard is becoming lost in process. It's one thing to go to a good school. It's quite another to graduate and use the frameworks and lessons to build success in your life equivalent to the success of the institution that taught you.

As someone who learns best in a classroom, my father constantly reminded me of his belief about education. He was proud and even grateful for what investing in my private catholic education K–12 did for me and my brother. He believed it was the best thing he and my mother ever could have done for their family. But after postgraduate degree number two, he said, "Baby, the longer you are in school, the dumber you get." It was his way of saying what good is it to have all this education when you cannot use it to serve and impact those who need it most? How and when are you going to find a way to simply say what you need to say to the people who want to hear it plainly from you? One of the last things he said to me was, "You have no idea the value that rests in your head. Share it with the world; believe in your ability to apply it to situations and communities that matter to you!" In other words, apply your knowledge.

Intellectual capital is not just exclusive to book learning and limited to a classroom. Your NRID will reveal how you best process and apply information. An example that will forever remind me of this fact happened while working in New Orleans with a client I grew to love and respect tremendously. Every week I would write a report of the work I had completed and my suggestions for the road ahead. I would print out the report and set it before him with the expectation of going through it in intimate detail. What began as a frustrating experience grew into a treasured one. My client was an elder of the community, with years of history in solving complex issues, yet he wouldn't even look at the report. Instead he would look at me and say, "Tell me what you see." I would answer and he would ask more questions. After a few months of this I asked one of the board members why it was that my reports were never read in our meetings. She looked at me and asked, "What makes you think he can read?" Flabbergasted, I refused to believe this leader, the manager of a multimillion-dollar business that spanned generations was illiterate. I summoned the courage a few weeks later to ask him. He simply replied, "I know how to read what matters, Pamela—people. Besides, with all them degrees, I thank God I can pay you to read for me." Again, not all knowledge occurs in the classroom and application of whatever knowledge you have obtained benefits you and all who are in the midst of the growth that ensues.

#3—Human Capital

Human capital along the NarrowRoad is what you do with your strongest talents that distinguishes you from others in the market place. While they say time is money, it is really everything, not just money. Along the NarrowRoad, your money is a simple equation: your time multiplied by the wage you are able to negotiate. Human capital is more than that because you are not paid for the twenty-four hours you get every day. Valuing your talents that you are the strongest in creating with beyond the value the market gives you is how you expand your time value of money. Imagine if we used our best as currency in our community and learned to build systems for exchanging with it? Everyone in their unique way would feel valued and learn to even strengthen their strength with practice. We would learn how to better exchange value with others, and business would not be a dirty word. Neither would corporate, which really is just a group with shared interests working together.

Despite constant compliments and encouragement for my ability to publicly speak, for most of my professional life I did not like to play to my core strength. I thought it was weak, and not tangible enough. My focus was on the numbers, hard core analytics which at first I was not very good at. I remained silent while studying and trying hard to build an expertise in an interest versus playing to my strengths. That changed when a superior/mentor finally sat me down and said, "You know all the things you hold as most important are things that I can train and hire someone to do, but the thing you are most adept at is something that must come from within. You know how to engage the client in ways that build trust and confidence. That is not a trained skill, that is a God-given gift. Use it, please."

The biblical scripture that promises your gifts will make room for you materializes quicker when you play to your strengths, those innate gifts that maximize the value of your human capital. Your time on the road is a gift, use it in ways that create income and other opportunities. There is a room for it in our community, trust me.

#4—Social Capital

Social capital along the NarrowRoad is who and what you connect with; it is what you are most passionate about, the things you will take extreme risks for. Social capital is best utilized in vulnerable areas of your life, the places where you have a need that cannot be addressed without assistance. This is where who you know matters in pursuit of the life you desire to live. With social media and twitter the benefit of social capital is obvious but the value not so much. How does who you know elevate your standard of living? What economies of scale can you build with the tribe you currently live with?

Throughout history it has been the tribe, the group, the fraternity or sorority that builds scale to the vision. It is the collaboration with others that converts value into a chain that can support the needs of the masses, give birth to a vision whose time has come, and breath life into a dream that needs support. Social capital is what takes you beyond the survival mode of life, but not without risks. There is work involved in building a great group capable of scaling your current existence. You have to trust and believe and wait and speak up. Your social capital along the NarrowRoad is centered on your fourth role in your NRID. Vulnerability around this role and responsibility is what brings authenticity to your social networks, it is what maximizes the value in the relationships near and dear to you. Hiding the need in this area reduces this capital into the shadows of your life. Social capital is reduced to a who you know, and how you know the game we all in some networks play. But for social capital to be of best and highest use to you, you must expose more than the places and spaces you are great.

As an entrepreneur for more than ten years, who loves to help people, this lesson in maximizing the value of social capital was hard for me. On the surface social capital mistakenly is confused as a popularity contest, yet once you venture deeper it evolves into an exercise of who can consistently be who they say they are. Leaving corporate America for a venture of my own was a daunting task itself, and staying within a network who was not pursuing the same dream became for me almost impossible. I remain grateful to my friends and family in my social networks who taught me best this lesson I share with you. My innermost social networks connected to my dream and invested in me in ways that I needed it most—even when I was unwilling to ask.

Social capital when utilized for the asset it can be is sacred. Along my NarrowRoad journey I have had the privilege of working with formalized social networks who for the last century have remained together in the support of each other and their community. Known as the "Divine nine" these organizations set an example of what social capital can do when passed on for generations. While not a member of any one sorority I remain proud and inspired by the passing on of traditions and legacy so needed for past, present and future journeys. Having worked with the oldest black fraternity, I have seen first hand the beauty in building a net that works across the country and the community; it is a beautiful thing indeed. Again I say social capital when pursued beyond the surface is a capital worth saving and investing in.

#5—Spiritual Capital

Spiritual capital along the NarrowRoad is found at the very places where there seems to be no road left to continue. Throughout my journey I have found that people use the term "spiritual" to distinguish themselves from organized religion. As the creator of the NarrowRoad I find it important to share that I am a theologian and while biblical principles and narratives are infused throughout the journey, they are to guide the path to thinking deeply about what it is you truly believe in your very own unique context, situation and story. My research revealed that almost everyone when faced with a financial challenge or uncertainty in some way closes their eyes and believes that it will eventually be ok, it will work out somehow, some way. What one believes in for the situation to work out is up to the believer. The act of doing it is when you leverage Spiritual Capital. Some have more than others, most have just enough. This faith is the currency that fills the voids between what you can do, think see, or speak and what is beyond you.

Grow Your Belief, Grow Your Assets

Along the NarrowRoad a "genesis," where you start on your journey toward the promise inherited in your life. The journey begins with your family business model. An exodus is the choice you make to become the owner of your journey, your business model. Your genesis is experienced in your childhood as an incubated asset of the family business. This is the financial model you grew up in that taught you the context of certain degree of freedom. Your exodus is the steps you selected upon departure from the incubator of the family business to a business of your own. Each person may start at different genesis points and make different exodus choices that lead to different terrains in the wilderness, but what is clear is that "experience, training, and personal effort can take you the rest of the way," said Robert Sternberg, an American psychologist. "A major factor in whether people achieve expertise is not some fixed prior ability but purposeful engagement." Where you begin does not have to be the end in your NarrowRoad all you have to do is learn how to navigate the future with the capitals you have in your possession.

The knowledge of a growing belief in your abilities and "purposeful engagement" could be used to address the income gap that exists within our society. While this gap has never seemed more complicated, it has never been simpler. I believe the wealth gap is more important to watch and has a lot to do with the number of people who are ill equipped to move an idea from a dream to a mission that can be executed to create wealth-producing outcomes. I believe the wealth gap has everything to do with the low financial- and business-literacy levels throughout our society.

Redefining Wealth with Legacy

Wealth is the value of everything a person or family owns, minus any debts. Income is what people earn from work but also from dividends, interest, and any rents or royalties they are paid on properties they own. In theory, those who own a great deal of wealth may or may not have high incomes, depending on the returns they receive from their wealth, but in reality those at the very top of the wealth distribution usually have the most income.

In terms of types of financial wealth, the top 1 percent of households have 35 percent of all privately held stock, 64.4 percent of financial securities, and 62.4 percent of business equity. The top 10 percent have 81 percent to 94 percent of stocks, bonds, trust funds, and business equity, and almost 80 percent of non-home real estate. Since financial wealth is what counts as far as the control of income-producing assets, we can say that just 10 percent of the people own the United States of America.

Many people associate wealth with power, and while they are two very different things, they do share some similarities. Power has to do with the capacity to realize wishes or reach goals, which amounts to the same thing, even in the face of opposition (Russell 1938; Wrong 1995).

Wealth can be seen as a "resource" that is very useful in exercising power. That's obvious when we think of donations to political parties, payments to lobbyists, and grants to experts who are employed to think up new policies beneficial to the wealthy. Wealth can also be useful in shaping the general social environment to the benefit of the wealthy, whether through hiring PR firms or donating money to universities, museums, music halls, or art galleries.

Certain kinds of wealth, such as stock ownership, can be used to control corporations, which of course have a major impact on how society functions. Just as wealth can lead to power, so too can power lead to wealth. The wealth distribution can be seen as the main "value distribution" within the general power indicator I call "who benefits." When I asked thousands of people to define seven key words, I got thousands of definitions, one of which was "power," I asked eight billionaires how they defined power, and I got one definition. The definition was actually an applied equation.

Grow an Appreciation of Your Assets; Grow Your Own Definition of Wealth

The opportunity that existed in the Promised Land was to build a definition of freedom through ownership of inherited land according to their own terms and an ongoing covenant with the God they believed in.

Many of us business owners are slow to react to the need for a change in our operating system. So what does this mean? Do we need a new title, a new territory, a new degree, or more hard work? Not exactly. It means we need to work toward building our definition of wealth. One example would be to consider a new cross-functional operating model, one that values more than just your most recognized ability to do things—more than what you are paid for. It requires a view of your life that includes all the capitals within your portfolio of assets. It means believing that you are uniquely designed and resourced to pursue opportunities to expand, grow, and build a legacy in ways that include wealth creation. Your NRID is the key to aligning your assets with the strategies required to design a new cross-functional operating model and work smarter on your personal pursuit of your inherited portion of the promised land.

To build an operating model whose chosen destination is wealth, we must work to define wealth individually and then work within the guidelines of this definition. This way your road will contain incremental improvements in the way you value your time and organize around that value. A valuation along the NarrowRoad is a review of all three of your financial statements (balance sheet, income statement, statement of cash flows) including all five of your capitals. Over time your valuation will produce positive net worth or increased levels of it—a position that begins every journey to real freedom.

Getting to enough is the first step toward creating a forward march toward your Promise. Having learned your lessons in the terrains of the wilderness (see chapter 8), now is the time to be about the business of you it is after all an inherited business. Make it better with choices that reflect your financial valuation. How will you mine those lessons, experiences, observations, and messages? Welcome to the business of you! You are the most valuable asset you will ever possess. The promise is just a reflection of the whole you, the value of every last capital in your in your portfolio. As with every aspect of the NarrowRoad, there are dimensions. This step along your journey is no different. Action is the difference between pursuit and possession. Possession requires resources that are informed with who you are, where you are, and where you desire to go from here. Believe in your actions, believe in what you do and how you do it and you will grow your assets used for creating wealth.

Strategy Is Important

By now you should have gotten my point that this wilderness experience is not a new thing in our communities. Finding a strategic way to break the pattern of wandering is. What is the best way to do this? Connect your pattern with the patterns that came before you, put things into a perspective that enlightens your point of view beyond just talking about it to thinking it through. Use your capitals to fund your pursuits.

Lessons Learned on the NarrowRoad

Setting anchor points allows us to monitor the progress of our pursuits. Along the NarrowRoad we anchor in two places, our genesis and our next level of Promise (definition of freedom).

Learning how to navigate beyond the wilderness requires an understanding of timing and acumen around the levels of promise.

The three levels of Promise are simple:

Level one is the distance from survival to freedom, survival being living from paycheck to paycheck and relying solely on yourself. The outcome of a life of survival is that of leaving this world with good intentions but little fruit for those who journey after you. You did everything in the storm by yourself and so it all dies with you. Freedom is the ability to make choices based on things in addition to cost, to have the ability to save and build a life you can structure to include a generation beyond you. The journey is shared and so are the lessons learned and wealth created.

Level two is the distance from freedom to growth —freedom in this case has different degrees, one being middle class (desiring to earn your way ahead), the other being the middleman (desiring to own your way ahead). Growth is the outcome that comes from partnering with opportunities and dreams that share your pursuit of legacy wealth and owning a stake in the success of pursuits other than your own.

Level three is the distance from growth to expansion, growth in this case is the now proven personal productive strategy that can be used to expand your legacy beyond where you can see. Expansion is when you have become the master of all the talents you have at your disposal to reap harvests that will last for generations to come. Your legacy is one of leaving harvests in fields you have not planted seed to future generations.

Here is how we are going to survive in the wilderness:

- [ ] **Step one:** Write your simple vision.
- [ ] **Step two**: Run with it
- [ ] **Step three:** Have patience. Be present in the meantime. Have faith it will work out as you work towards it.
- [ ] **Step four**: Recognize your life is the light in the future's dark places. Work your faith until it reveals itself to others and yourself.

Reviewing the Five Forms of Capital along the NarrowRoad

The following will help you better understand the NarrowRoad you're traveling. Answer as honestly as you can (if you're honest with yourself, your road will narrow to a path conducive to your success). There are no right or wrong answers, even if they don't match everything you've read in this book—remember, for legacy wealth to be attainable, it must be defined by you and the choices you understand.

1: List assets that fit in your cultural capital portfolio

____

____

____

2: List assets that fit in your intellectual capital portfolio

____

____

____

3: List assets that fit in your human capital portfolio:

____

____

____

4: List assets that fit in your spiritual capital portfolio:

____

____

____

Chapter 8: Life, Liberty, and the Pursuit of Promise

Elements of promises that are realized remain consistent across journeys. Ranging from the colonization of America to the pursuit of freedom post-slavery, there is an invitation to believe an opportunity exists that results in a migration of some kind, a delay of some type that causes one generation to wander and die and another to commit to stop wandering. Successful leadership, battles, victories, and the possession of Promise; however, it may be defined, is often a leap of faith. Often, impassioned and forceful words precede the first exodus from slavery/poverty to emancipation/emergent freedom, and death precedes the second exodus from fear of the full responsibility of freedom to unblinded faith about inherited ownership and the wealth that can ensue.

The Genesis of America—A Land without Promise (Yet)

America was thought of as the land of milk and honey, yet most of its first settlers died from starvation. It was seven long years of repeated failure for the first group who desired to build a land of the free enterprise in Jamestown, Virginia. The early settlers had left what was familiar to start up a new business venture with the intention of building wealth from mining gold. That was their plan. Armed with the history that colonization was nothing new to English settlers, it was believed that America would be no different to take possession of. But the starving times kept killing each new group of determined settlers. This was the early 1600s, and in Jamestown, the creature comforts of organization, policy, and free labor—otherwise known as slavery—had yet to be established.

Leadership, tools to build a nation, and resources to feed the first movers were the common issues in the wilderness of early America. They began with a collective model, believing that if they pulled from one storehouse they would have enough to succeed. Unlike the Israelites whose supply came from God, the expectation was that the settlers would replenish the storehouse from the harvest that came from their work in the land. Over time, successful colonies were established.

A Dream Deferred—Hopes and Dreams Migrate through Ways and Means

While in the financial wilderness and the Promised Land, there is work to do in the field. The work is what enables each generation to reap the harvests that lead to the time of promise. For the Israelites the wilderness was organized into four standards (lion, man, ox, eagle). Each standard contained three tribes and one group of Levites. The centermost tribe, the tribe of Levi was divided into four groups, one for each standard. The tribe of Levi was the only one not to receive an inheritance within the Promised Land because their responsibility to God was too great to manage both responsibilities. They were the tribe responsible for the building up and the breaking down of the tent of witness that held the ark of the covenant that sat in the center of the camp while wandering in the wilderness. When the time came to leave the wilderness, they were the first to enter Jordan, followed by the lion, man, ox, and eagle standards, in that order.

Once the framework for America was established, it worked similarly to the wilderness operations. Those tasked with the building up and tearing down of the plantation field in times of seed, planting, and harvest did not receive an inherited portion at harvest time. Unlike the Levites, though, these persons were slaves in America and were not acknowledged for their abilities to navigate the tent of witness located in the center of the field. "By 1860, there were more millionaires per capita in the Mississippi Valley than anywhere else in the United States."

"Slaves' humanity was not restricted to a zone of 'agency' or 'culture' outside their work. When slaves went into the field, they took with them social connections and affective ties. The labor process flowed through them, encompassed them, was interrupted and redefined by them. Slaves worked alongside people they knew, people they had raised, and people they would bury. They talked, they sang, they laughed, they suffered, they remembered their ancestors and their God, the rhythms of their lives working through and over those of their work. We cannot any more separate slaves' labor from their humanity than we can separate the ability of a human hand to pick cotton from its ability to caress the cheek of a crying child, the aching of a stooped back in the field from the arc of a body bent in supplication, the voice that called time for the hoes from that which told a story that was centuries old."_

Throughout America, slaves in faith sought out God's witness and protection as they toiled the land, believing that as they worked to reap harvests for their masters, that would finance the building of the world's fastest growing superpower, one day they would too inherit their Promised Land.

Their invitation to believe in the Promise came some 150 years ago in the form of emancipation. Preceding emancipation was a civil war that slaves themselves supported to fight in exchange for their Promise. Once the Red Sea of civil war was crossed, exodus into the financial wilderness was a reality that took generations to navigate after various types of attempts to possess the land. Generation after generation, this population of Americans migrated into the four winds, seeking ways and means to transition from being a creator of wealth for the nation to a wealth creator for themselves.

The Emancipation Proclamation was an executive order issued by President Abraham Lincoln on January 1, 1863, as a war measure during the American Civil War to all segments of the Executive branch of the United States. It proclaimed the freedom of slaves in the ten states that were still in rebellion, thus applying to 3.1 million of the 4 million slaves in the United States at the time. The Proclamation was based on the president's constitutional authority as commander in chief of the armed forces; it was not a law passed by Congress. The Proclamation did not compensate the owners, did not itself outlaw slavery, and did not make the ex-slaves (called freedmen) citizens. It made the eradication of slavery an explicit war goal, in addition to the goal of reuniting the Union.

Eighty-five years later, in July 1948, President Harry S. Truman signed Executive Order 9981, which declared "that there shall be equality of treatment and opportunity for all persons in the armed services without regard to race, color, religion, or national origin."

The march for the Promise began. A key marker in the Civil Rights movement is the historic Brown v. Board of Education verdict won by unanimous agreement in 1954. The victory declared that segregation in public schools is unconstitutional. A first step in legally defining the bridge to independence via equality, this ruling paved the way for large-scale desegregation. This victory was won by NAACP attorney Thurgood Marshall. This was his dream, to level the playing field. To get to emancipation, Thurgood's idea was to plant "seed cases," which in this case were the eleven lawsuits he filed on behalf of African American children in the South and the District of Columbia.

"Five of these cases—from South Carolina; Virginia; Delaware; Washington DC; and Kansas—finally arrived at the Supreme Court in 1952 under the heading of Brown." Marshall had what might seem to be an extremely simple view of the Reconstruction Amendments—the 13th, 14th and 15th Amendments—designed to secure racial equality.

A year later, in 1955, in Montgomery, Alabama, Rosa Parks ignites a second step toward independence by refusing to give up her seat at the front of the "colored section" of a bus to a white passenger. Her action defied a southern custom of the time. In response to her arrest, the Montgomery black community launches a yearlong bus boycott that forces the city to desegregate the buses on December 21, 1956. This victory is the spark that ignites the flame of Reverend Martin Luther King Jr., a new minister in the area who would quickly ascend to become a leader of the movement along a different road toward the same promise.

In 1963 more than two hundred thousand people joined the march on Washington where participants from around the world would listen to the now-famous "I Have a Dream" speech, very little of which was written on paper.

Almost a year later President Johnson signs the Civil Rights Act of 1964. "The most sweeping civil rights legislation since Reconstruction" prohibits the discrimination of all kinds based on race, color, religion, or national origin. This law, unlike Brown v. Board of Education, also provides the federal government with the powers to enforce desegregation. The walls of Jericho had started to come crumbling down.

The late 1960s also had its fair share of dark places, beginning with 1965 when in February, Malcolm X, black nationalist and founder of the Organization of

Afro-American Unity, is shot to death presumably by members of the Black Muslim faith, which Malcolm had recently left in favor of orthodox Islam. Similar to the battle of Ai (Joshua 8:1–35), the Nation of Islam in their quest for change had divisions within.

A month later, in Selma, Alabama, a march in support of voting rights is stopped at the Pettus Bridge by a police blockade. The incident is dubbed Bloody Sunday by the media as fifty marchers were hospitalized due to police brutality. This march is considered the catalyst for pushing through the voting rights act five months later on August 10. This Act makes it easier for Southern African Americans to register to vote. The voice of an oppressed people was beginning to be heard.

The year 1968 marks the battle that brought the fire and the pain. On April 4, hours after he preached he had been to the mountaintop, thirty-nine-year-old Martin Luther King is shot and killed as he stood on the balcony outside his hotel room. President Johnson signs the Civil Rights Act days later prohibiting discrimination in the sale, rental, and financing of housing. America legally opened the gates to the Promise in the land.

The pursuit of promise has many dimensions. Its wealth is passed on by remembering. Take some time to connect the dots in your part of the wilderness to look back down the road you are traveling, and I promise you will find a glimpse of light in whatever dark place you find yourself in.

A vision leads to thoughts about "how," which leads to actions of "what" and messages of "why"; these result in outcomes of great value over time. The visionaries, thinkers, doers, and speakers consciously and unconsciously live lives that connect across history to create a legacy that is passed on for generations. The wealth is created when you build from Lessons Learned from our history. What about our history enables you to move further in your life pursuit?

When the legacy connection to our life pursuits is forgotten, the opportunity for wealth creation is not passed on to the next generation, it is stored up like hidden treasure waiting for someone to remember the legacy. The cycle begins again from the beginning—such as a fight for education, equality, and laws that support the winning of battles fought and won before.

It is for these reasons the NarrowRoad is a guide for elevation.

- ❑ Elevating our history to the guidepost it can be
- ❑ Elevating our legacy to wealth
- ❑ Elevating our pursuit to ownership
- ❑ Elevating our journey to life purpose

We are born into an ongoing legacy narrative, and we make it what we choose. It's a series of unconscious and conscious choices that become our dialog with ourselves, our community, and our world. Our history is a roadmap of what is possible when an idea evolves into a dream, becomes a mission, and builds into a shared system, a way of life that becomes the vision for the future. It is in this way history can become prophesy. The pattern continues when the roles people play pass from one generation to the next—and Moses becomes Joshua, Dr. King becomes President Obama, Michael Jordan becomes Kobe Bryant, and Shirley Chisholm becomes Hillary Clinton.

Your idea becomes your granddaughter's vision. This pattern of progress spares no one and offers the invitation to contribute where you see fit to keep the wheel of progress turning. All you have to do is stay connected. And connection is an interesting thing. It in itself forms a pattern within a pattern. The idea of the American Dream was improved by the European aristocracy who determined that to build America as a land of the free, you needed ownership amongst the pioneers; the right to life, liberty, and pursuit of ownership became the strategy to keep the progress wheels moving forward. Ownership requires work, and the work in the beginning was the mission of the slaves, who, while working for their masters believed that, despite harsh conditions, one day would result in freedom. The work required a structure to build to a scale necessary for freedom as a nation, and those system builders who structured the order of the land into the Bill of Rights and the Constitution further moved the wheel of progress forward. Finally, the vision emerged after a few necessary negotiations via amendments, and the workers and the experts could pursue the promise in this land. Still not on equal footing, the wheel continued to turn: ideas—dreams—missions—systems—visions.

From which turn of the wheel did you come? This is our shared history. I came from workers, mission-driven people who were determined to do for others long enough to earn the right to do for themselves. I also come from experts, masters who, with the assistance of workers, built wealth in this land that passed on for generations. Their lives are the models of the visions we look to when reflecting on our history. We often jump from idea to vision when reviewing history, leaving necessary elements out of the story. This leads to a repetitive cycle similar to a wandering in the wilderness seeking treasure that once again has been lost due to lapses in memory of the key elements of progress.

The elders reveal the hidden truth when they repeatedly say the way forward is back through. The adults reveal their order when they claim the youth have not a clue about what to do to move forward. The youth reveal their need for organization when they claim the elders know not what they are taking about. We all in some way as a result rely on blind faith to somehow turn these disperse ideas into dreams, these dreams into missions that build into systems to reveal the vision we are all hoping for.

Our history is a prophecy, and a prophecy is a vision for an appointed time. My quest with the NarrowRoad was to put the pieces together so we will cease to blindly walk along the roads that have been laid before us. We must open our unique eyes and once again with purpose begin the journey of taking our ideas to experts to convert into dreams that will be taken on as missions and build upon with systems to reveal a vision whose time has finally come.

There is no need to rewrite history. There is a need to unearth its hidden treasure in your life so that you can pick up the torch of your legacy and move it forward to a system of wealth creation that will over your lifetime become a model for legacy wealth.

Reviewing your Life, Liberty, and the Pursuit of Promise

The following will help you better understand the NarrowRoad you're traveling. Answer as honestly as you can (if you're honest with yourself, your road will narrow to a road most conducive to your success). There are no right or wrong answers, even if they don't match everything you've read in this book—remember, for legacy wealth to be attainable, it must be defined by you and the choices you understand.

1: The first promise along the NarrowRoad is the ability to sustain yourself with the talents you have been given. This is measured by income and your ability to afford your needs. Reflect on your current financial situation and how close you are to fulfilling this promise.

____

____

____

2: The second promise along the NarrowRoad is the ability to leverage your relationships with others to build a life you desire. This is measured by systems, groups, and structures you collaborate to get what you want. Reflect on your current lifestyle and how close you are to fulfilling the wants you desire in your life.

____

____

____

3: The third promise along the NarrowRoad is the ability to grow your financial independence beyond those who came before you. This is measured by your partnerships, strategies to get to the next degree of freedom for your self and your generational advancement in life when compared to your parents and grandparents. Reflect on your strategies for financial independence how confident you feel in your present pursuit.

____

____

____

4: The fourth promise along the NarrowRoad is the ability to pass on your wealth wisdom to the next generation through investment of at least one of your five capitals. This is measured by those who pick up your torch and carry your legacy narrative forward. Reflect on the ways your leadership and vision impact those who are journeying the road behind you. What will be your legacy narrative for them be?

____

____

____

5: The fifth promise along the NarrowRoad is the prayer you have for the fourth and fifth generations you will not live to see but will benefit from legacy of your pursuit. What is the future and hope you desire for them and how can your faith plant a seed to carry it through?

____

____

____

____

Part 4: Our Roadmap

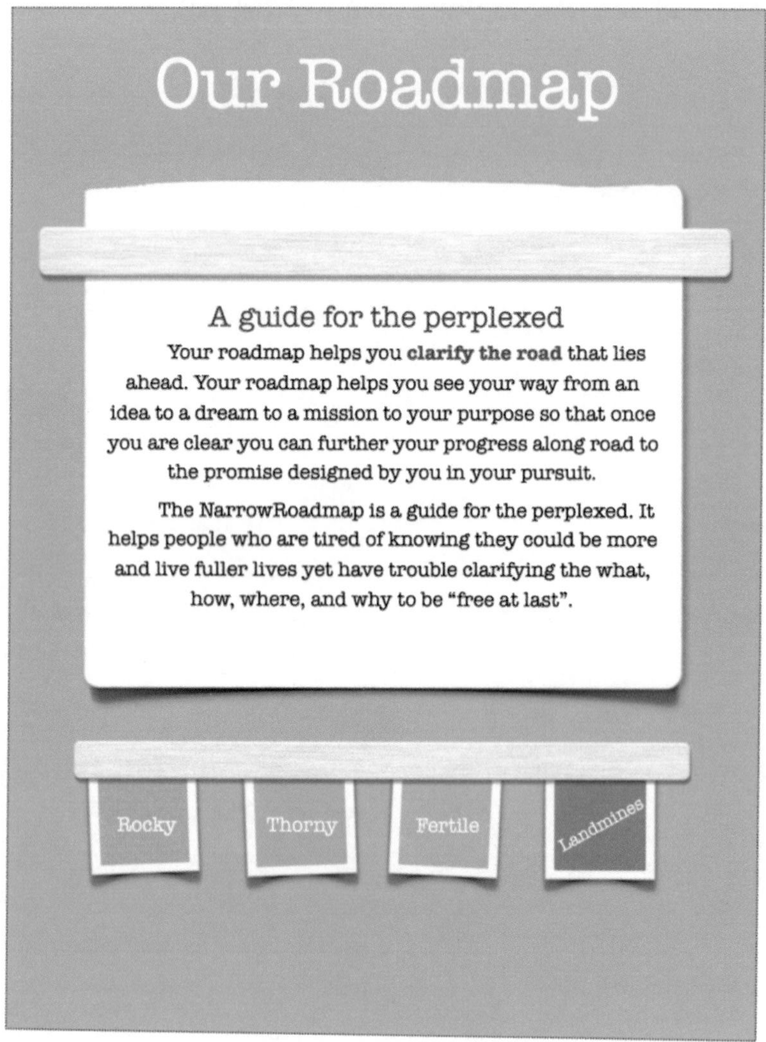

Your roadmap integrates the four quadrants in a pathway. When applied to your identity, it becomes a roadmap custom-tailored to you.

My roadmap began with the affirmation of what I do best. For as long as I can remember speaking was the gift that made room for me. I would talk to my great grandparents as a little child and I remember their eyes would light up when they listened to me. My father, mother, and brother would listen and tell me people need to hear my voice. Classmates at Wharton would pull me aside and say, "You have a gift. When you speak, people want to do something." I used this talent to sell car stereo equipment at Circuit City to pay for college. I used this talent to sell the hardest product out there, which is money in my role as a banker. I used this talent to collect terabytes and terabytes of data from people for the creation of the NarrowRoad. I use this talent to motivate people across the country about their unique abilities to build legacy wealth.

This talent remained buried for years. I only valued it when others told me it was valuable. My focus stayed on what it was I could not do (the weakest quadrant Q4) at the level of my peers. This is what hampered my confidence (quadrant 2) and kept me wandering in the financial wilderness. I kept exploring how I could see my way to success in classrooms (my strongest Quadrant 1). Yet every time I let my talents make room for me, amazing things happened.

A large bank heard me answer a not-so-random question on a panel in Atlanta and sponsored me to speak at events across the country. Executives and leaders would hear me speak at these events and hire me to speak to their employees. Believers would hear me speak and invite me to meet their pastors, priests, and rabbis, who invited me to preach and teach to their congregations. Parents and teachers would hear me speak and invite me to speak to their schools and children.

While this was great I still would focus on what it was that I could not do Q4. I felt there was more for me and my inability to ask for the help I needed made me feel stuck and incapable of adding the real value I desired.

Your roadmap helps you clarify the road that lies ahead. Your roadmap helps you see your way from an idea to a dream to a mission to your purpose so that once you are clear you can further your progress along road to the promise designed by you in your pursuit.

The NarrowRoad roadmap is a guide for the perplexed. The people who are tired of knowing they could be more and live fuller lives yet have trouble clarifying the what, how, where, and why to be "free at last" once they have created their NarrowRoad map.

True freedom is when you own your path to promise and take it. If your recall the Bible verse in Matthew from which the NarrowRoad is named—"Enter through the narrow gate. For wide is the gate and broad is the road that leads to destruction, and many enter through it. But small is the gate and narrow the road that leads to life, and only a few find it."

My grandfather Alphonse Jolly said to me, "Baby girl, in life there are many options but only one choice that is right for you—choose wisely." (He also said, "Never be an options girl only be a choice girl when dating men," but that's a story for another guide along the NarrowRoad.)

Life is filled with options. You can do what you to do, be who you desire to be, focus on the road ahead, and learn from vast amounts of teachers along the way. Choose these things in a sequence that leads to your promised success and live the life you were promised. That is the belief embedded in the NarrowRoad. What you will find is that parts of your road's vision have already been "made plain." You have just yet to connect the parts to your roadmap to chart a path to wealth.

Wide is the Gate

The wide gate leads to destruction because right actions done in the wrong sequence can cause so much damage that it makes your vision dim in the dark places you can't understand, it destroys your confidence, it devalues your talents, and allows you to speak against the desires of your heart because of fear. Many wander around these stuck points in the wilderness year after year. Things could start off great and then loop back into chaos, confusion, avoidance, and a life that does not speak your truth.

But Small Is the Gate & Narrow the Road

Small is the gate that invites you to define grow, create and build wealth your way. You see along your road through a unique lens that is culturally biased by the legacy narrative you have inherited. Your grow confidence along the NarrowRoad by the opportunities designed to sharpen your skills in your pursuit. You create income needed to fuel the fire of the business of you by unearthing your talents and deploying them wisely and you build a life you desire by sharing the load of freedom with others who are willing to engage in your truth. The narrative created by these identity specific statements become your roadmap the life you desire. Only few find it because, as my grandmother says, "It's hard to see the full picture when you are posing for it." Hard to see it, hard to believe it, hard to consistently pursue its reflection, hard to admit that the full picture of your legacy wealth includes so much more than you. Remember seeing is believing and so once clear my belief is you will take the NarrowRoad that is uniquely created by you and evidenced with your roadmap.

Enjoy this phase of your journey, my friend. If you need additional assistance and would like to navigate your roadmap with fellow wealth-building friends, navigate your way to www.mynarrowroad.com/roadmap and let's begin your path to making your journey along the NarrowRoad plain.

Chapter 9: The Financial Wilderness

Legacy wealth is a journey that connects you with the past, present, and future. It assigns you the role of designer of your path and pursuit to take possession of your promise. If it sounds out of this world to you, it is—society does not think this way. Society's focus is right now, in the moment, all you; which is often unconscious of the wealth systems that function beneath your focus on what is just a snapshot of you.

What your NarrowRoad journey reveals is that legacy wealth is within you, like a seed planted in the ground. It is often the lays dormant, silent but remains a potent driver that carries you at places along your wealth journey assisting you when you find yourself uncertain or confused. The primary objective of legacy wealth is to move you forward, to be the constant resource that fuels your fire as you navigate the areas of your life that initially appear as uncharted territory but are really roads that have been chosen for you to inherit access to. Your pursuit along these roads, whether you deem successful or not is the harvest of legacy wealth investments that were made generations before you. Equally important to remember is that a promise of Legacy Wealth also resides beyond you; as it spans for generations. There are some experiences along the road that leave seeds for those coming behind you.

Everyone contains within them the desire to pursue the steps necessary to chart a path to legacy wealth. The problem is that few find the steps, and even fewer take them. I can say this with certainty because I heard it through out the country as I interviewed men, women, business owners, and pastors about their financial futures and desires to go further beyond their parents, mentors, and leaders in their community. This is why I felt led to create a NarrowRoad so that one can tap into the desires within themselves and that of those who came before you to chart a path toward a promise you will live to see. I want us to get beyond the story of the past pursuits of the promised land to the narrative of how we are to take possession of it! The Promise really is up to how you manage, operate and choose to lead the business of you. The first assignment for the business of you is to get out of the financial wilderness and onto a path you choose. This path is a wealth system.

A wealth system can be created in one generation and preserved in two. But it takes three generations to create legacy wealth, four to grow it, and five generations to expand it. No matter what level of wealth you accomplish, it can all be lost in one generation by simply discontinuing the legacy narrative that spans across generations.

Constants and Variables

In creating the NarrowRoad, I found there were key patterns that appeared as I looked for models within narratives, legacies, people, and groups that had found their respective promised lands. A common thread that every journey has are constants and variables. A constant is something that lasts and matures and evolves over time, such as a vision of what your legacy will be or a specific desired outcome. Variables are situation-specific elements that can shift as you need them to, such as strategies, actions, and messages. The NarrowRoad framework when viewed as an equation accounts for these constants and variables via frameworks.

Studying the successful pursuits of both life and business I have found that the 80/20 rule where 80 percent business is same and 20 percent is different, really is true. In the case of the promise of wealth creation, the 20 percent is based on your perspective, your vision of what is valuable, and worth investing a lifetime to pursue. Your perspective is in many ways your cultural equity, the value you place on what you have been able to see throughout your lifetime. The depth of your perception, the vision of what is possible is a determinate of how far down the road of promise you can afford to look. For most people, seeing is believing. For a few, the ability to believe first, expecting to see things come into plain view is a unique talent. Unearthing hidden stored abilities to believe and see is what I call cultural capital. Everyone has it, but not everyone uses it as a legacy wealth investment.

The gift of sight is one of the essential elements of Promise. Seeing brings about the ability to believe a desired thing is possible. Sight and vision along the NarrowRoad are two very different things. Vision is a pool of cultural capital that affords you the distinct ability to see through to the next level of wealth creation, your next level of Promise. How you use it to deepen your perspective is the gift, it the investment of it.

Along the NarrowRoad there are four types of visionaries. Each one investing a unique perspective. The answer to the question how far down the road are you looking, is first answered with the first role of your NRID. The first role of your NRID is how you initially see things. You are either a pure visionary, where vision is your strongest role, a thinker-visionary, where thinker is your strongest role, a doer-visionary, where doer is your strongest role, or a speaker-visionary, where speaker is your strongest role. Your strongest role is what shapes your perspective. (see grid at the end of the chapter for more insight into your legacy perspective).

The Terrains in the Wilderness

Along the NarrowRoad™ there are four different terrains in the wilderness. The patterns I found within the wilderness journeys of people I interviewed and observed was best described in the narrative of the path from the wilderness to the promise land. Along the road to promise there are four stages of development. This is where for me the promise land narrative meets the lessons in the parable of the sower. In the parable of the sower a farmer sows seeds on four types of ground, Rocky, Thorny, Fertile and Land. There were four different outcomes for seeds that fell in his field. Those outcomes are the four stages of development one must move through their journey to promise.

Along your pursuit of the promise you travel through these four terrains to get to an understanding of who you are. This way of understanding of who you are builds the confidence that overcomes much of the fear that forms roadblocks along your pursuit of legacy wealth. For the Israelites this took 40+ years of wandering to get to the point of navigating past their fear. For you should you decide to take the NarrowRoad™ it can be much shorter. The shorter path is called a quantum leap.

You are who you are, your identity is unique to you. Sometimes the pursuits of your life will like seeds in a field, hit rocky ground and your big ideas appear to quickly proceed just as you imagined until abruptly everything stops, and you get the opposite of what you expected which is a polite way of saying failure. Sometimes your pursuit will grow through challenges of thorny ground where everywhere you turn there is one snag after another delaying your pursuit of your dreams, forcing you to pay attention to what is important. Other times your pursuit will hit fertile ground where what you dream of takes root and grows upward reaping stages of harvest, and sometimes your pursuit will hit the land-mines, where outside influences, like birds of the air, grab your pursuit and turn it into something unintended and even in some instances undesired.

Everyone has dreams and your unique dreams are like seeds that, when planted in fertile ground, grow into the fruits of your promise. Not all pursuits end up in that part of your field. The other areas of your field contain lessons that result in beneficial experiences that the wilderness is designed to teach you. It is important to view the wilderness this way so that as you approach the roadblocks found in rocky ground, thorny ground, and landmine patches along your life journey you do not stay stuck. Being stuck limits your choices concerning a pursuit of the Promised Land and, if not careful, leaves you wandering in patterned circles of the wilderness for a lifetime, leaving your legacy promise for the next generation to sort out the details.

Building a solid foundation, based on your unique legacy perspective, overcomes rocky ground. Understanding how to overcome your insecurities about independence and growth will get you past the thorns. Knowing how and when to multiply your talents reveals the harvests in your fertile ground. Having a strong sense of your mission and purpose overcomes the landmines. All of these strategies are pursuits along the wilderness journey of the NarrowRoad™.

The way that the NarrowRoad™ model helps you build a journey of strategic pursuits is that these terrains happen to everyone, and like the four turns of the wheel, your unique identity guides you to effectively navigate past these terrains in the wilderness your way. Forming a roadmap based on your choices about your legacy, independence, talents, and life purpose narrows the road to become your life strategy. Owning this plan for your life is how you will get to the Promised Land, however you define it; despite the obstacles, both seen and unseen, that occur in everyone's life journey to building legacy wealth.

Legacy Is a Cross-Generational Narrative through the Terrains in the Wilderness

Legacy implies inheritance; inherited wealth is ownership of something passed from generations. Everyone in some way is left something to carry forward. For some it is lived experience and for others it's knowledge, social acceptance, financial resources, or an idea; everyone is an inheritor of something. No one is left out of this passing of the torch from one generation to the next. One may not value or choose to look for their inheritance, but everyone gets something.

There are different ways to define and ways to distribute inheritance. The pursuit of happiness, the American dream, and the Promised Land are all inherited narratives that over time come to fruition. It's all different ways of saying the same thing: wealth is an outcome we all desire for ourselves and our families now and in the future.

The notion is that wealth can be created in one generation and preserved in two, but it takes three to arrive at legacy wealth; the fourth generation grows the opportunity, and the fifth generation expands it, can be traced throughout history. Look at the #1 soup company in the country, Campbell Soup; they are a four generation company. While there are many other soup companies that compete for your purchase, Campbell Soup gets the benefit of the doubt every time as a trusted source of good food. This gives them the market to grow in terms of offerings and varieties. Another to consider is the non-bank institution CIT financial. Within its 100 year history, five generations, they have expanded investment models in to communities where many financial institutions refused to lend to.

The city of New Orleans is a perfect example as the oldest inhabited place in the nation. Five generations have lived there; it is rich with cultural, intellectual, human, social, and spiritual capital. It demonstrates the power that can happen when families stay connected and pass on traditions over time. While the poverty on the individual level was high at the time of Hurricane Katrina in 2005, the tourism business was five billion dollars strong and employed many of the impoverished people to produce elements of their culture. Collectively, the service, hospitality, culture, music, and food produced an income capable of sustaining a city known to others as "the big easy" and a source of a good time rich in cultural history.

Dr. King was born in 1929, the year of the last big financial crisis since the one we experienced in 2008. Born into a middle-class family created by children of sharecropper parents, he was protected from the abject poverty and harsh realities many African Americans faced in what would be the Jim Crow South. Within his small circle in Atlanta, he was protected from the lynchings and restrictions of access to education. Educated in the North, he was able to see and experience things many other people of his skin color had not. He navigated the thorny ground of the wilderness for years trying to unify his ideas of freedom with the dream of equality and justice. His wanderings in the wilderness are chronicled in his books, most notably Where Do We Go from Here: Chaos or Community?, published in 1967, a year before his untimely death. Written on a retreat in Jamaica, Where Do We Go from Here was King's analysis of the state of American race relations and the movement after a decade of US civil rights struggles. "With Selma and the Voting Rights Act, one phase of development in the civil rights revolution came to an end."

Why We Can't Wait, written in 1963, is a book that began with his letter in the Birmingham Jail. It speaks to the power of nonviolent protest and why now was the time to pursue the promise of freedom. As a second generation, Rev. Dr. Martin Luther King sought to preserve the wealth his own family passed on to him in the legacy narrative of Promise that still educates, inspires, and teaches people on a global scale to this day.

Malcolm X's upbringing and experience was a contrast to King's. Born in Omaha Nebraska, his father was killed early in his life. He was the son of a mother prone to depression and as a result spent a great deal of his life in a system ranging from foster homes to various prison facilities. His primary education as a result came largely from his experiences, prison, and the streets. Intuitively brilliant, similar to King, he found his voice within the halls of the invisible institution—the black faith community. Malcolm's legacy illustrates the elements and effects of rocky ground with his voice catching fire and sparking ideas in the minds of others who picked up where he left off to clarify the dream for independence. In many ways as a first generation he sought to pass on a wealth legacy of owning your position in society and defining it for yourselves.

Wealth Is a Series of Financial Decisions

These wealth decisions build, grow, and expand over time with savings and investments. The more aware you are, the more prepared you become to pursue your journey.

Today, society's definition of wealth is limited to material possessions or money. I have learned that one of the main obstacles to building wealth is a lack of literacy of the real meanings of key financial terms. Society's adapted definition excludes the core meaning derived from its original old English word, weal. An expanded understanding of the word wealth is "an individual, community, region or country that possesses an abundance of such possessions or resources to the benefit of the common good is known as wealthy."

Economists define wealth as "anything of value." The United Nations' definition of inclusive wealth is a monetary measure that includes the sum of natural, human and physical assets. Natural capital includes land, forests, fossil fuels, and minerals. Human capital is the population's education and skills. Physical (or "manufactured") capital includes such things as machinery, buildings, and infrastructures.

To personally define wealth, one must know how to value his or her possessions. And possessions increase or decrease in value over time.

Decisions Are the Difference between Creating Wealth and Becoming a Wealth Creator

Your financial decisions determine how far down the legacy wealth road you travel. The first stop of any journey is that of a creator of wealth. Your time spent working benefits the long-term vision of someone paying you. In this light, you are a creator of wealth and a generator of income for yourself. The next stops along the road reveal the different degrees of freedom that are necessary to move to balance the equation to support your own wealth desires. The NarrowRoad teaches the principles of business and finance so that you can elevate your life to whichever degree of freedom you choose. Wealth is built in stages and phases of development. The further down the road you go, the more opportunities you are exposed to. In life, there are many options, but the choices of a wealth creation are limited to a few specific tools to build, grow, and expand the value of your holdings.

The Terrains in the Wilderness

Think of the four primary roles of The NarrowRoad as cornerstones—Vision, Thought, Action, and Speech. These four cornerstones are connected with the central element of Outcome to lead you out of the wilderness onto a path toward your promise of legacy wealth as you define it.

The primary objective of the NarrowRoad is to assist journeyers in the pursuit of their promise which resides beyond the financial wilderness. We all post our initial family business experience (Genesis) take an exodus that lands us in some terrain in the financial wilderness. The journey's one finds themselves navigating is somewhere between two of the four cornerstones. These journeys are categorized as the four terrains in the wilderness—rocky ground, thorny ground, fertile ground, and landmines. Exploring these four terrains of the wilderness will help you determine the answer to the question, where are you in the Wilderness?

Terrain #1—Rocky Ground

Rocky ground is the distance between the beginning and the end of the NarrowRoad equation. Located between vision and speech, or quadrants 1 and quadrants 4, this is the area where tough lessons are learned that help you frame your perspective and give you insight into the areas where you are not yet ready to build the life you desire as you see it. The Rocky ground is the place where you overcome your blind spots—the places where you and only you see it clearly but others do not share in your point of view. One of the difficult realities about wealth creation is that it is a collective process. You can get rich on your own, but if you want to scale it to wealth you have to collaborate with systems and groups of people who may not see it as you do. The Rocky ground is the terrain in the wilderness where you run up against these realities about wealth. The rocks are the reactions and responses to your unique perspective concerning the order of things, the risk and the return of your idea, what is praiseworthy and what needs additional prayer, and where you still need to be enlightened to build a life based on your vision.

The Rocky ground in anyone's wilderness journey can be painful yet purposeful, if you allow it to sharpen your gift of sight and clarify what you really want. Some stay stuck in the rocky ground of the wilderness by shifting their attention from one idea to the next at the first appearance of rejection or lack of acceptance. These people become very defensive; unable to cooperate and build with others, yet they desire to do big things that impact the masses. If this is you or someone you know, my suggestion is to listen intently to both the idea and the reaction because there are patterns in both. Don't let critical (even when supportive) feedback that gets you nowhere get lost in translation; there is a message in this terrain for you. To find out the specifics of your rocky ground, visit mynarrowroad.com/rockyground.

Lessons Learned from Rocky ground

To leave the rocky ground areas of your path to promise one must understand that every sharing is an exchange for which there is a hire and a reward. Sharing an idea is essentially asking another to hire your eyes for the reward of seeing it through your perspective. Additionally, one must understand that there is a difference between prayer worthy requests and praise worthy requests. Prayers worthy requests are shared with those who already believe in your ability to lead your idea to fruition, they understand the order in which you accomplish things and are confident in your pursuit. Praise worthy requests are those that have been matured from an idea into something more concrete and can stand up to the scrutiny that those who currently have not your eyes to see, need to really understand and believe in what is becoming your vision.

If you find yourself wandering in the rocky ground of the wilderness my advice to you is to take inventory of your rejections, study your NRID system of success, and chart a path further down the NarrowRoad along the lane best suited for you.

I find most entrepreneurs who struggle to make consistent income wander in the wilderness along rocky ground. Big ideas, big desires to share it with others, are soon followed by repetitive disappointments. When equipped with their NarrowRoad™ Identity I am able to shine light on the details of the path that lies ahead for them, if they take the time to write their vision and make it plain.

Terrain #2 - Thorny Ground

The Thorny ground sits between your first and second quadrants; this terrain exposes the challenge areas that rest between how you see and how you think. The distance between these two elements of your identity is a narrow one that initially triggers confusion and overwhelms. The benefit of thorny ground is that it organizes your way forward by forcing you to prioritize the areas of your journey where you must clarify and learn how to grow your idea into a dream. Dreams are things you can share. Dreams, once understood, build confidence in pursuing the road ahead for both you and others.

Some of your ideas are meant to go further down the road, despite the rejections and criticism. You know this is the case when you still are led to pursue it. You now have the courage to take an idea that you believe in to fruition. History has proven that dreamers are remembered and followed. The journey is an independent one, at first. You have to build the confidence required in you. To take your idea to the next level will require you to navigate terrain #2 in the wilderness, the valley of the thorns. Thorns are those pesky little details that choke and snag your idea in the places that are either not useful or beyond the scope of your current understanding. Remember an insecure mind cannot learn along the NarrowRoad. Your pursuit must have a level of understanding and knowledge to be successful. What survives the thorns is what turns your idea to a dream.

Key things to move your idea to a dream:

1. **Write the vision and make it plain.** Unify your perspective with proof others can appreciate for this to happen void of exaggeration and in the moment improvements, it must be written down.

2. **Learn from what your challenges reveal to you.** During the proving process, I found that everyone must learn and grow somewhere to pursue a dream. For me my growth required additional degrees, I needed a classroom to build confidence in my pursuit of my dream for my community. For you it may be other things but learn what you must to continue your pursuit of your dream. Don't waste time faking it, skip a step and potentially defer ownership of your dream to the next generation.

3. **Obey the rules that govern the fruition of an idea into a dream.** In my research a pattern that became ever so clear was that every successful dreamer I found had to obey three rules: a dream has to be tested by others, a dream has to be understood by others, a dream has to be able to be pursued with others. If your dream does not abide by these parameters you're not being obedient to the rules of a successful dreamer. True independence requires partnership with expertise at some level.

4. **Understand the power of organization**. The last thing that it takes to move an idea to a dream along the Valley of thorns is organization. You have to prioritize and organize the elements of your dream so that others can share experience, understand, and visualize that which was uniquely given to you. Every dream has dimensions, things you can pursue right away, and others that will take more time, more people, more planning, and more learning to bear fruit. This was a valuable and painful lesson along my journey, while I like to learn in intense situations that resemble drinking water out of a fire hose, I found that not everybody agrees. I had to organize the dimensions of my dream for it to flow beyond the thorns into the minds, hearts, hands, and eyes of others.

The thorns are tough, they challenge you in areas that you need it most but are often reluctant to admit it.

Malcolm X's journey along the valley of the thorns revealed that perhaps there was a way to share his dream with others he had not previously considered. His vision for the financial independence of his people was a relevant and necessary one, his method evolved over time with the challenges he faced along his journey. At the end of his life, he left a legacy that black student unions across the country picked up and to this day are working to carry it through. We don't all get through each of the terrains in the wilderness but a dream that gets through the thorns is almost always remembered by those who take the time to learn the key elements of an idea whose took the time to prove its potential to bear fruit.

Terrain #3 - Fertile Ground

By now you have expended a lot of time and attention to the details that trip you up most along the journey. You are ready for the next terrain along the NarrowRoad™ which is fertile ground. Fertile ground sits between your second and third quadrants, this terrain exposes the fruitful harvests that exist between how you think in how you act. The distance between these two elements of your identity is what dreams and missions are made of. When in this phase of your journey good things happen, doors open for you, and your unique talents are appreciated for all the hard thinking and searching you have done to get this far down the road.

The benefit of fertile ground is that it builds both confidence and faith in your choices and abilities to pursue your dream.

Dreams are opportunities you can share. Dreams, once understood, build confidence in pursuing the road ahead in both you and others. This terrain is when you take your dream and do something about it. Fertile ground is when you have something tangible to do about what you see and believe. This means you are ready to come above ground with something the world can consume - your talents are on a mission to bear fruit with your dream. You are creating what will be a viable solution to a problem others can identify with and pay for. This is called a harvest along the NarrowRoad™. Harvests are returns on your seed investments of time, talent, and treasure.

Harvests come in three increments — 30 fold, 60 fold and 100 hundred fold.

A 30 fold return feeds you consistently when you put your best, strongest talent in the area most ready to engage with it. Your first level of harvest comes from the talent that is most affirmed by others (often in your third quadrant); it is the gift that makes room for you without any real effort.

A 60 fold return is when the exchange of your talents can benefit you and others. This 2nd level of harvest requires you to collaborate and in some cases partner with others who can see how your mission can benefit their interests if they join in on the pursuit of your dream with you. This second level return on investment is where you take responsibility for your ability to grow your talent with the expertise of others who may or may not know you and they may or may not share your total vision. The compounding interest created in the joint venture is what brings this medium fruit to full harvest.

Lastly a 100 fold is a return brings value for everyone in the wealth building equation — those that came before you, those that will come after you, and anyone who's a part of your wealth group (the people involved in helping you bring the dream to full fruition).

When you, tangibly, pursue your dream it becomes a mission. There are steps that have to happen to take a dream to a mission.

1. **Go into Exile**: The step feels like a period of exile, this independent phase of the journey supports what you need to get confident about what this dream really is, what this dream really can do, and your role in bringing it to fruition. You must own the direction of the dream for it to be your mission. It was six years between Dr. King's success with the Birmingham Boycott and the March on Washington, there was a period of exile where he had to build confidence in this part of the mission for his dream.

2. **Seek Affirmation**: The second step is a welcome shift to a place of affirmation. Seek out confirmation of the strengths best used for your mission. Getting people to affirm your dream means that people appreciate the intention you are bringing forth with your dream. You need words from those that matter to you to affirm your mission's importance, relevance in society, reliability of deriving outcomes. Everyone does not have to agree with your mission but some group has to; remember wealth is a group process.

3. **Take Responsibility**: the third step is responsibility. Responsibility, in this instance, is the willingness to deal with what the mission requires to move from theory to praxis. For dream to become a mission, you have take responsibility for it, you can't leave it up to chance, you must think it through. A dream has to contain substance and evidence, enough so that you feel confident that it can be accomplished. If not solely by you, then you at least have an understanding of what and who is needed to bring the dream to fruition.

4. **Unblind your faith**. The last part of turning a dream into a mission is faith. It's not blind faith, but faith unblinded by the rocks and the thorns that got you here. It's a level of confidence that fuels your belief that when you do what you know how to do with your talents and opportunities, God will do what you cannot (often

through the partnerships and collaborations with others) to see you through to the harvests further down your road.

When Rev. Dr. Martin Luther King stepped up to the podium at the march on Washington, he was prepared, he had a speech that outlined what he wanted to convey. It was Mahalia Jackson who interrupted his perfectly prepared message with the urging "Tell them about your dream! Martin, tell them about your dream!" That partnership with those who stood with him in his moment gave him the fire to fuel his faith that yes, it was time to share his dream, yes, he was ready, yes there were supporters who would take hold of the vision his life and legacy had made plain and run with it. The rocks and thorns were tough but at that moment he was ready, his mission was to share with the world in a way that they would remember.

Faith is a required part of any person's dream to truly manifest what you have been given eyes to see. After you have navigated the fertile ground that preserves the promise of harvest, you now must walk through the land mines. The journey along the NarrowRoad™ continues.

Terrain #4 - Landmines

In the parable of the sower the land is where the birds of the air pick up the seeds before they even have a chance to take root. Along the NarrowRoad™ the journey begins with navigating beyond the rocky ground, lessons from this terrain help you order your steps. Further down the road is thorny ground that clarifies your idea into a dream, this is where you are organized and confident of the pursuit ahead of you. The Fertile terrain is where you come above ground to multiply your talents by pursuing opportunities that are ripe for harvest. Landmines sit between your third and fourth quadrants, this terrain exposes the trigger points that exist between how you act and how you speak and engage others. The distance between these two elements of your identity is what defines the road ahead of you, the wealth within you, and the life you desire to live. When in this phase of your journey you are vulnerable when you least expect it, people love you, words matter, and you find your truth and are given the invitation to exert the courage to share it. The benefit of the landmines is that it trips you where you need to focus and forces you to face the true desires of your heart and deal with what it's going to take to attain them.

At this point you now understand your mission, you have been affirmed in your talents, you have taken responsibility to grow, and have even taken leaps of faith to prove the time now for you to bear fruit. What the world is asking you now is this; everyone has a mission and dreams, What is your purpose? Why you?

If you don't know the answer to that question, then you will be picked apart by the birds of the air, affectionately called the landmines. Landmines are society's interests that will overtake your mission and change it to whatever they want. If you are not clear of your purpose and how your mission builds to scale, you can get confused and become distorted by the chaotic act of being all things to all people. Without a purpose you can be convinced to try to do more than you are capable of doing and fears of both success and failure can lead you to focus on the potential threats to your survival. Your mission could become a hustle if you are not clear about what your purpose is. There are 4 steps you must take in this terrain of the wilderness. The reality is to survive taking your mission beyond the land mines means arriving at the real purpose of your pursuit of promise. Here are the steps to get beyond the land mines to the legacy wealth journey you were promised.

1. **Choose to Rebel**: The first thing is to rebel. Not fight, rebel. Fight means to take part in a struggle, rebel when facing the landmines means to resist the control others try to place on your full expression of your vision. My great-grandmother would always say "resist the devil, chile, and he will flee, don't waste all that good energy fighting something you already won —own what you see." You must rebel against society's pressures that will say you cannot do this, you are weak in this area. Rebel against others beliefs that you're not good

enough, the idea that you don't know enough, haven't done enough. Enough! You know what you have been through; you know what you have been preparing for. This type of rebelling is against something specific — the business as usual mandate that is no longer working for you and people you care about. Scaling your mission is your purpose, and elevating your standard of business is the way to do it. Overcoming some fears and weaknesses is how you do it. In the land mines these words, accusations, and questions pick at your fears because at first most people are afraid of what your success might bring about for them and you. No one wants to be left behind. So, if you have done what you have needed to do, resist the notion that others know more about the promise of your mission and scaling than you do.

2. **Advocate for yourself**: The next step is advocacy, what is it that you need? To be successful amongst the land mines you must learn to advocate for yourself. Unlike the challenges you faced with the thorns these distractions in the land mines of your journey are not working together for your good. You must know the specific needs of your mission so that your purpose is sustainable. Specific details such as your budget, weak points in your system, and what is required for you to sustain this part of the journey beyond just you making it happen is the way to navigate beyond the landmines to your realized purpose. This step helps you find your

voice. It was after all a shout that brought down the walls of Jericho, it was a message that survived generations that encouraged those willing to pursue the Promised Land inspire of the giants that inhabited it. Your promise requires that you advocate for yourself as confidently as you can advocate for others.

3. **Understand your position.** An understanding is more than an idea, more than a dream, this is faith that has been worked and has been successfully bearing fruit. This confidence comes from an understanding of your strengths and talents that when used in specific ways address both the needs of others and you. This level of substance and understanding is what you rest upon to demonstrate why now is the time for your mission to move to a specific purpose, a specific persuasive role in the community that needs you. My grandfather would always say, "1% doubt and you are out baby, stand firm in what you understand".

4. **Let your life speak your Truth**: The last thing to overcome the landmines is to allow your life to speak your truth; the reality is that you have seen the promised land in this journey, but you are not there yet. You are on your way. Don't be afraid to admit it. Truth opens doors for people who want to join you. There are more followers than there are leaders in this world. You will be amazed at the number of people desiring to share your pursuit of purpose to find the meaning in their lives by

assisting you in the pursuit of yours. So, no, you don't have all the funding, no, you don't have it all figured out, no, you can't do it all, and no you don't see from everybody's perspective, but you do desire for the right people to join your journey and share in the fruit of the purpose of your pursuit. It took me a long time to get comfortable enough to pass through this landmine. What I learned along my jolly journey is that everyone looks for a weakness in those who are strong but not everyone wants to hurt you with what they find, many, if you let them, will help you get further down the road, it's part of their purpose to help you along the way towards their promise. PLEASE, don't block your blessings; let your life speak its truth. You have come a mighty long way, your lived experience is a message your community needs to embrace. Wealth is a group process, a shared experience that includes both weaknesses and strengths.

This is a strategic pursuit of the journey beyond the circular pattern of the wilderness. For your legacy wealth journey to be strategic the pursuit of your promise includes experiences in all of these terrains. While some areas of your pursuit are collective, to build the confidence required to build wealth your way, most of them, initially, are individual. This is the solo part of your journey, beyond the wilderness is where the fun begins. From here you can participate in the group process of the path to promise.

Chapter 10: The Four Roads in the Wilderness

Which best describes you?

- ☐ I have a vision, but when I try to share it with others, they don't see it as I do.
- ☐ I have a vision, but I seem to run into obstacle after obstacle when trying to pursue it.
- ☐ I have a vision and knowledge of how to pursue it, and I am working on it and receiving success but I know there is more for me to do.
- ☐ I have a vision and the knowledge of how best to pursue it. I have experienced success but get overwhelmed at the idea of building it to scale with others.

Picking up the torch is a unique opportunity everyone can consider along their life's journey. While to some it may not seem like it, it is far easier to build on something existing than to start from scratch. Building from scratch can appear to produce quicker results in the short term, but in the long term, the obstacles you face in working with an established way of doing things are the very things that will ultimately slow you down in your new venture—they are just further down the road. Life, similar to business, is really 80 percent the same and only 20 percent different. The 20 percent is your perspective. Is your vision based on an idea or have you taken the time to enlighten yourself with the paths that have come before you?

The Way Forward is Really Back Through

It is for this reason we begin the NarrowRoad journey looking at what has come before our entry gate to the NarrowRoad. There is nothing new under the sun, as the saying and scripture goes; time and chance happen to all (Ecclesiastes 9:11). Your time and your chances improve significantly if you take the time to anchor your leg of the journey to a destination beyond prior pursuits. What you desire to ultimately do will begin with greater equity when you take the time to pick up a torch. A torch is an unfulfilled dream of someone before you, it can be someone famous or someone special to you.

For America in general, and specifically African Americans, the height of the Civil Rights movement was a time of exodus into a wilderness that prepared many for the great battles that stand between a willingness to fight and the actual actions required to take full possession of the Promised Land. Ownership is responsibility, and without a strategy that looks beyond paying the mortgage to taking full possession of the land, the Promise can slip between the gaps across generations. The legacy perspective can get lost in translation if not connected to a community understanding.

Within America, African Americans share a distance of approximately 150 years from slavery. In the midst of this shared distance is a choice of four roads: rocky, thorny, fertile, and filled with landmines. Your families, regardless of your ethnicity or race, decided to migrate post-emancipation to build, to earn, to learn, or to expand. This split is in the roads taken beyond emancipation defines the various degrees of freedom that exist in every community today. Within the African American legacy narrative resides valuable business lessons for anyone desiring to pursue financial independence that passes on for generations. We face financial emancipation past our first eighteen to twenty years in what I call our family business. This genesis period teaches the core elements of what we use to build a life for ourselves.

The first inflection point we all face in our lives is how we extend the legacy of what our parents and grandparents invested in us.

The reason the legacy pursuit of freedom and equality of the African American community has so many business lessons, is that African Americans are the only segment of the population in America who first were capital before they made capital. Their ancestral roots are just not a matter of memory, history, legacy, and tradition, they are a matter of public financial record. African Americans came to America on the balance sheets of emergent plantation business owners desiring to build a better life for their families by any means necessary. Within this pursuit was the use of slavery as a business model. Besides the land, the African slave carried the most value in the financial statement of early America. They were the human assets whose work created the products America used to build tremendous wealth in one of the shortest time periods in history. Theirs is a legacy that began as extreme creators of wealth for others. Their transition to becoming wealth creators for themselves is a multigenerational lesson in business and finance that impacts the entire nation if not the world. The history of the African American journey demonstrates the elements of the NarrowRoad method for legacy wealth. The vision, the thoughts, the actions, and the messages all lead to outcomes that create, build, grow, and expand what the business of living is all about.

It's history. In the Bible there are two parts: the Old Testament, which speaks of a future time, and the New Testament, which often reflects on a prior time. Christianity, Judaism, Islam—all faiths stem from the same source—God's promise to Abraham. We all serve an important role in history, whether it is to move the lever forward from survival to freedom for ourselves and others or to move beyond freedom to a new height of awareness of what is possible, what is necessary, and what is needed.

It is in this way our history is one of the best teachers about wealth and purpose. There are patterns in history that can remind us of where we are, where we are going, and what we need to pay attention to so the road we are traveling in our lifetime is in many ways smoother than the road traveled by those before us. It is in this way that history is prophecy.

One of the most pivotal books I read along my journey was Generations by Neil Howe and William Strauss. These two brilliant historians and strategists went back in history and studied the connections between the generations. Their research revealed a pattern they call a saeculum. The authors posit a pattern of four repeating phases, generational types, and a recurring cycle of spiritual awakenings and secular crises, from the founding colonials through the present day. History essentially repeats itself every four generations. Strauss and Howe went back to the 1500s and found that every fourth generation we begin again a cycle. From this research they created a predictive modeling component and wrote a second book called The Fourth Turning. It was here they used history to predict what would happen now. The Fourth Turning was written about "right now" more than twenty-four years ago. It is remarkable how accurate it is detailing how our society would reach a point of crisis, of meltdown, so it can build itself back up again.

Things are crumbling around us, revealing what we must pay attention to. Our economy is revealing its breaks in the system, our financial services industry is revealing its need for more accountability on all levels, and our government is revealing the need for greater participation to encourage a more perfect union. In the narrative of the Israelites, it was Joshua, not Moses, who led the pursuit of the Promised Land. It was the third generation, not the second, who followed suit.

Delays in the inevitable are not denials to a promise whose time has come. It is due to my love of research, history, and these two aforementioned books that my journey has been enlightened with the eyes to see key patterns in our history that reveal the importance of going back far enough to pick up some of the deferred dreams of the past that have been fertilized in the pursuits of those before us and are ready for harvest now.

This pattern in history is one that repeats over and over again once you understand its principles. There is nothing wrong with dreaming big. Big dreams are what has gotten us through the stuck points in history. The most recent big dream came from our resident dreamer Dr. Martin Luther King Jr. His dream left a fifty-year imprint in our historical memories. Similar to his biblical mentor, Moses, he spoke of a Promised Land that he had the privilege of catching a glimpse of, but he would not get there with us. Dr. King's pursuit of the big dream of freedom ultimately led to a life, however short, in pursuit of a purpose of economic equality for all people in America. Near the end of his life he remarked that he felt like he had led his people into a "burning house" that he discovered from the road he had traveled when he reviewed the expanse he navigated.

The pattern of history is a revealer of purpose if you take the time to connect the dots. Throughout your NarrowRoad journey, history will be your teacher. Together we will connect the dots to reveal the choices and decisions you must make to navigate beyond the financial wilderness everyone's life journeys through. The NarrowRoad in this way views history as a valley of dry bones. When called together, bones can breathe life and build a mighty army for you to pursue your purpose within your window of opportunity.

Our lives span four generations. A generation is roughly twenty-two years. Our window of opportunity to influence and contribute financially to the movement of history is often condensed into forty years. Two generations of time is what we have to navigate though the financial wilderness to build up a necessary reserve to fund the possession of a promise we each have uniquely inherited.

The New Testament consists of letters ranging from believers who were dreamers to believers who wanted to actualize the promise of the dreams in their communities. These letters, called gospels, were good news that believers navigating the wilderness of life could reflect on. These letters shared the history of what happened so the hearers of the Word could believe in what would eventually come again. Because it was promised.

History does not change. We, however, can change our perspective of the value of our history. We can use it as the good news it is to chart our path leveraging the proof of concept the lives of others represent in the present day questions we have now.

Building a reserve to fund the possession of the Promised Land in your lifetime is not just composed of money. Money is really just time multiplied by a wage. Your time is also converted into other currencies that are equally if not more valuable. Throughout your NarrowRoad journey we will explore all the currencies you have available to you and ways you can exchange them to navigate your unique wilderness to get to the promise you have chosen to spend your life to pursue.

At this time in our history, whether you represent a first, second, third, or fourth generation, we are all on this journey together. The best is always yet to come, and history promises it. Those with the audacity to realize it know some dreams have been deferred, and they take the time to learn ways past dreams can create advantages for their visions. I am one of those people and you are a beneficiary of the results of my legacy wealth pursuit.

It is in this way the legacy narrative continues. So let's journey further down the road together and pickup a torch or two to further light the path of prophetic history.

Reviewing Your Functions and Roles along the NarrowRoad

The following are questions to help you better understand the NarrowRoad you're traveling. Answer as honestly as you can (if you're honest with yourself, your road will narrow to a path conducive to your success).

There are no right or wrong answers, even if they don't match everything you've read in this book—remember, for legacy wealth to be attainable, it must be defined by you and the choices you understand.

Question 1: Which best describes you?

- ☐ I have a vision, but when I try to share it with others, they don't seem to receive it as I do.
- ☐ I have a vision, but I seem to run into obstacle after obstacle when trying to pursue it.
- ☐ I have a vision and knowledge of how to pursue it, and I am working on it and receiving success.
- ☐ I have a vision and the knowledge of how best to pursue it. I have experienced success but get overwhelmed at the idea of building it to scale with others.

Explain your choice of description:

____

____

____

Question 2: How does history enlighten your legacy wealth perspective?

____

____

____

Chapter 11: Getting out of the Storm

Getting out of the Storm Is Easier Than Most Think. As you recall, the storm is when you attempt to do everything yourself, avoiding asking for help from others to build the life you desire. Getting out of the storm begins with a shift in wealth perspective, which is the first step. Answering the key questions: How far down the legacy-wealth road are you looking? And in which direction? These questions lead you to the realization of what is the furthest future point you can afford to see. Is it now, next week, next month, next decade, or next generation? Is the depth of your perspective limited to qualitative ideas that sound good, or have you journeyed far enough beyond your imagination to clarify the quantitative realities of the legacy you desire to pursue?

Seeing clearly is believing. Getting out of the storm requires a vision of the legacy you desire to create —not an idea of it, not even a dream, a mission, or a message but a vision, something that takes perspective and time to develop, time that began before you even existed.

Once you have gained a wealth perspective, the second step to getting out of the storm is to develop a financial strategy. We all begin in the field of opportunity somewhere, and without a strategy for exit, the field is more like a wilderness. Without a strategy, it's hard to know how you are going to get out of the financial wilderness everyone sometime in their lifetime finds themselves in. For many, the financial wilderness is a place that one wanders in for the length of their forty-plus-year career.

Finding your way out of the financial wilderness has less to do with options and more to do with understanding your choices. The NarrowRoad defines poverty as a life without options. While some choose to focus on the struggling of poverty in America; my research and lived experiences have led me to the conclusion that while yes, there are some people struggling with poverty, more of us then we realize are struggling with financial oppression. Financial oppression along the NarrowRoad is defined as not understanding your financial choices. There really is nothing new under the sun; time and chance do happen to us all. A strategy is what helps you take full advantage of the window of opportunity you have in your lifetime. A strategy helps you navigate beyond the patterned circles of financial chaos and confusion so that the road beyond the financial wilderness is uniquely custom-made to your intended pursuit. You begin a strategy to get out of the storm with the second step along the NarrowRoad™.

Building wealth requires that you first commit to the decision that wealth is for you. What's next is to make your vision of it plain, with a strategy that creates your unfair advantage.

With a strategy in place that you understand and are confident about, you are now ready for the third step—assessing your current position in the financial wilderness. After you have chosen to get out of the financial wilderness and committed to your decision to exit the financial wilderness, and defined the level of wealth you desire to pursue, the third step is to uncover the resources you currently have to execute your pursuit of what you desire most. This is the point where you come to fully understand and appreciate the business of you. We are all in business. Anyone with a financial statement is in business. In business, there are various stages of engagement. Once you decide to leave the financial wilderness, it becomes time to elevate the standard of business you are currently engaged in to align with the legacy you desire to leave and the wealth you desire to create. Welcome to your mission. Later you will learn how you are necessary, talented, and needed.

Once the mission of the business of you is determined, you are ready for the fourth step of the NarrowRoad™ method: building your personal wealth system to ensure you stay on the NarrowRoad™. Your wealth system has been custom designed by you and your choices and includes a team of people with specific resources who are as committed to building wealth your way as you are. We will explore the key relationships you need to engage and/or develop as part of your wealth-building team. Individuals who will join your wealth journey are

- ☐ Friends who desire similar wealth outcomes
- ☐ Family who will commit to a shared desired outcome of legacy wealth
- ☐ A financial advisor you trust
- ☐ A financial institution in whose corporate mission and vision you believe
- ☐ Messengers who speak your language about wealth creation and legacy
- ☐ An accountability network that will encourage you to stay true to the legacy you desire to lead

The NarrowRoad™ method guides you to write your vision, make it plain, and run with it so with this type of team, you will be able to:

- ☐ Anchor to specific outcomes and build wealth your way
- ☐ Build accountability to stay true to the desires of your heart
- ☐ Chart a path toward growing financial freedom using your unfair advantage
- ☐ Build wealth together
- ☐ Create a life that is abundant in the present and sow seeds for harvest in the future

Following these steps and integrating the NarrowRoad™ method enable you to develop an integrated wealth system and get out of the storm. Once in place, you are set to order your steps toward a standard of living you desire, based on a level of financial independence you have defined and created a strategy to pursue.

It's a problem when both financial illiteracy and oppression blocks us from getting what we need. Many of us are wandering in the wilderness between "I should know this but have no clue how to find out" and "it's much easier to fake it till I make it."

Wilderness questions:

- ☐ What should be going on in your financial pursuit of freedom?
- ☐ What type of portfolio manager are you with your talents?
- ☐ What is your work pattern?
- ☐ What is your lifestyle pattern?
- ☐ What is your growth pattern?
- ☐ What is your investment pattern?

The fourth step of the NarrowRoad™ is finding your voice. This step is concentrated on the importance of defining your message in the building of your definition of freedom in the Promised Land. Within freedom resides an understanding that in order to stay there, you must maintain a standard of living that you desire. To do that you must build a better way to communicate what you want out of your life. As mother always says "ask not and you shall have not".

Your unique voice expresses what you feel. It is the energy that keeps the Promise alive and capable of transferring across generations. Yet many consciously or unconsciously remain silent, stuck between various stages of pursuits toward the Promised Land, waiting for the right time to speak our truth. That time comes when you accept that you are worth building with, investing in, and working with.

Businesses operate within markets, and markets serve as systems for exchanges. Working within exchanges, one abides by rules and regulations, policies and procedures. My big idea required an established system that connected individual and community desires for freedom. This system would make exchanges between faith and finance and work for the benefit of the collective pursuit of the promise of wealth. These systems are nothing new, they have been present in the world since the beginning of time, what was needed was a way for more of us to take ownership of our role within these interconnected systems.

The varying degrees of systems such as these are why McDonald's, for example, is a multibillion-dollar enterprise with mediocre hamburgers and the local sandwich shop often barely breaks even. Both desire to serve hungry customers, and both are in markets where there are hungry customers, but McDonald's is working at a different degree of freedom than the local sandwich shop. By degree of freedom I mean one's ability to do what they want when and how they desire to do it. In other words, the degree to which you can call and others will answer and ultimately follow. McDonalds has proven that if nothing else they will be consistent in their delivery wherever you are in the country. The new sandwich shop has some relationships to cultivate and those relationships determine the degree of freedom they can and will over time operate.

While studying at Oxford University, one of my favorite professors, Dr. Peter Shelby, said, "Without regulation there can be no relationship." Meaning the strength of a relationship is based on the boundaries it sets. Boundaries create the freedom to manage expectations and so that meaningful relationships can develop. "Without trust, there can be no exchange, and without exchanges there can be no wealth."

Everyone needs a system of some sort to collaborate with in pursuit of freedom.

To awaken to the economy of your life, you form a balancing act between your middle-class and middleman definitions. This is how you structure your middle road to the Promised Land.

Understanding Capital Relationships and Degrees of Freedom

The following story illustrates a useful way to consider the capital relationships in your wealth creation strategy.

Imagine you are getting married, and the love of your life is walking down the isle toward you. You stand waiting, looking down the road at what will be your life partner forever. As your partner walks down the narrow road, there is a beautiful green pasture, and a pool of still water. Just as your beloved gets ahead of the green pasture, your significant other trips over a glimpse of his or her shadow and falls into the pool.

What do you do?

The choices are obvious, their meanings not so much.

The first choice is to jump in and save your partner. The result would be both of you would be wet and ruined and all the people who came to see your cup runneth over with joy and thanksgiving would have to now wait for both of you to dry off and get cleaned up. Your partner would not feel lost and alone, but neither of you would be in a position to help each other by being stuck in the same pool. This is a perfect example of sympathetic capital; when faced with a choice to jump in and save someone, you run the risk of losing the very ground you have gained for yourself. (Sympathetic capital shows up when that same friend who has trouble managing his or her money calls you for help with the late rent or some other base expense. As you write the check, you know this is not a loan but another donation to your friend's poor speeding habits. It's not that you should not help; rather, you and your time and talents would be better served extending another form of capital relationship. Remember I said there were four choices?)

Next option would be to wade into the shallow end of the pool and motion to your severely embarrassed and sputtering spouse-to-be to venture out of the deep for help out of his or her unfortunate situation. Your partner would not feel lost and alone and would need to do something to get needed help. You would still have to clean up but not completely. This is a perfect example of empathetic capital. You know how it must feel, and you are willing to lend a hand in support of getting out of a bad situation with moderate risk that will be manageable for you. Empathetic capital shows up when you cosign for a loan or back someone up on a risk worth taking because you have been there and know the feeling. Helping in this way moderates risk but still puts you in a similar situation as the one you are helping. While this can work, there are still two other considerations.

The next is to look at the utter horror of the person who would have been your partner for life and begin to question why you ever would have selected someone so clumsy. You begin to unconsciously back up farther down the road and start to actually turn around and head for the door, preferring to eventually look for someone who would not embarrass you. This is a perfect example of apathetic capital. Apathetic capital shows up when you lose a sense of empathy and prefer to focus on your needs and the similar situations and conditions of others in the same boat. (A perfect example of apathetic capital is when you have done well for yourself and don't realize that none of the friends you grew up with are in your inner circle. You have "lost touch" and no longer have things in common. You don't think the same way and therefore have no need for knowledge of each other's situations. This type of approach in some instances is the best way individuals know how to get ahead. It fosters financial relationships that are good for the season they are in. But if the winds change and/or the season shifts, you may not have that group of friends. It's a choice along the string of options.)

The last choice of capital relationship is when seeing the love of your life sputtering and flailing in the water you run to the side of the deep end of the pool and instead of jumping in, instead of wading into the water, instead of running the other way, you hold on to the long-term desired outcome and see this current situation for what it is—a rock in the road. You hold out your hand and say, "I know this must be difficult for you, I know you are embarrassed, and you do look a mess, but it changes nothing about the way I see you and feel about you. It would not be in my best interest to jump in, but here is a way out of this situation. Calm down, grab my hand, and together we'll work to get you out of this pool and back on the road to the future and the hopes we have prayed for. While you get cleaned up, I will entertain our guests and plan for a way to laugh about this later." This is a perfect example of compassion capital, acknowledging the current situation and offering a strategy to get past the fear and resume the vision as it was intended.

Sympathetic, apathetic, empathetic, and compassionate capital relationships are all at work in all of our communities. Those of us refuse to engage in certain capital relationships can appear to be heartless or cruel, yet it reveals what part of the financial wilderness you are seeking to depart from and navigate to. Greater awareness of the impact each relationship type has on your individual wealth pursuit can lead to increased levels of trust and authenticity. Throughout my research many people referred to the "crabs in a barrel syndrome" and how active it is in community. Add Facebook and twitter and it increases the impact of peer pressure and acceptance. After engaging with thousands of people about their desires for a better for fruitful life, I have a different take on the crabs in the barrel. Instead of people not wanting others to get ahead and this feel the need to "pull them down" I believe a large part of it is not wanting to be left behind and begin afraid of expressing this. Getting out of the storm is as easy as expressing your truth to people who may not jump into the water with you but can in their own way give you the hand they feel most comfortable extending to help you further down your road. For those types of relationships you have to do your part in clarifying where you desire to go, what you know is important to get there, what resources you have available to fund your part of the journey and what resources you need to build to get beyond where you currently know. Everyone will not say yes and welcome you with open arms, my grandmother has a saying for that too — "rejection is God's protection, you are just as blessed with a yes as you are with a no so pursue them with equal vigor". I have been so blessed by the rejections in my life, they have taught me everything from how to pick better friends, to the importance of right timing. So I encourage you to overcome your fear of rejection. Armed with your NRID I can help you better prepare for both your future yes and no's.

The Truth about Sympathetic Capital — plan or you will fail

You know you are in a sympathetic capital relationship when there is very little long-term progress happens and the same problem resurfaces in regular almost predictive intervals. People in these relationships are intense in their feelings but less effective in their actions to do anything about these intense feelings. What I personally have found in sympathetic capital relationships is that those with the resources and good intentions eventually loose sight of an outcome and loose a control on their resources, namely time and money. I remember when I was in Boston speaking at an event about capital relationships there was an attorney who at one time was wealthy. Part of his purpose was to impact communities who suffered with extreme poverty. When I met him he has been pursuing this purpose without a plan or a team to support his good intentions for about five years. He had left his practice and went out to make a difference. The trouble was the vision was not clear to anyone but him, the strategy was not developed it just rested on his believe using what he knew how to do. His mission was heart felt but lacked a product and a business focus. Regardless of how accomplished he had been, no one valued him at the level he was accustomed to in the communities he desired to serve, so he began to lower his standards, his rules and regulations for relationships. In his desire to join in with the community he wanted to impact he remained silent in areas he should have spoken his truth about but did not fearing rejection from the very people he desired to serve. As a result within three years he had spent through his savings, his standard of business sunk to survival mode and he began to withdraw completely from his former associates and community. When I met him he was terrified of how he was going to afford responsibilities to his family and ashamed for having failed so miserably. Sympathetic capital relationships are akin to placing a Band-Aid on a gaping wound with the best of intentions but not the best business and financial acumen. My advice to him and those who experience bouts of sympathetic capital tendencies, (1) own your mission — where are your talents best contributed? (2) commit to being about your business within the problem you desire to in some way solve. (3) recognize the storm is a short term way to move people away from sympathy. Jumping in without the perspective you have invested heavily in is shifting your perspective to what is foreign territory. (4) Poverty is a big business, undoing poverty is an even bigger business. So why would you not be business minded in your pursuit of solving it? (5) Share what you know with those who will not only listen but follow your lead, sit on a board, create a how to manual for students following a similar path as you who come from the neighborhoods you want to impact. You have a value in sharing who you are and how you got to where you are, and why you want others to follow your lead.

The Truth about Empathetic Capital — timing is everything

Sporadic spurts of advancement followed by stagnant periods of low to no activity occur when there are high levels of empathetic capital. When the time is right, empathetic capital relationships are in abundance. Initiatives funded with empathetic capital never get completely finished, they address the tip of the iceberg, they build momentum for a season, and then they dissolve into good intentions not completely followed through. I see a lot of empathetic capital relationships in the non-profit world. For a period of a few years a specific special interest is the top on the list for funding and then as quickly as it began it ends, and those still focused are left to fend for themselves. When the feeling is gone, so is the support. This type relationship can be a spark that helps those committed to getting further down the road, but the ability to learn, save and invest in ways that will help in the future are key priorities to be mindful of while the focus and attention are on the topic or pursuit you believe in. My advice (1) focus on more then the ongoing support you are receiving now (2) learn the specifics of how the support you are receiving is being funded, structured, and maintained, (3) build skills in the areas most needed for longer term change, (4) build into your message a call for a deeper level of relationship with those willing to be committed beyond the empathetic period. (5) work with those lending an empathic hand to design milestones and outcomes beyond their participation in your progress.

While in New Orleans I shared a lot of empathetic capital. I so felt for communities desiring to rebuild. I shared what I knew and had for a period, it was those who took the time to ask me what should happen after my engagement ended are who developed the skills necessary to advance to the next level capital relationship. There is no passion in transaction and after the good hearted people go way you have to be about your business to succeed.

The Truth about Apathetic Capital — you must put on your mask first

Apathetic capital is very present when there are a select few rising stars who are surrounded by groups of people struggling to keep up within your community. At the onset, apathetic capital appears cruel and insensitive, but everyone in their own way must deploy a little apathetic capital. The word apathetic means showing or feeling no interest, enthusiasm, or concern. This is the position of someone solely focused on their dream, what they most believe in. To get from where you are to where you have never been have focus on your priorities for a period. I call this an exilic period where your primary objective is to build the confidence you need to succeed at what is most important to you. When we look at celebrities who make it big and seem to disappear for a minute, I believe they are building their independence so be able to grow into what they desire to be in community. And for a season that requires you to fly solo and take care of your needs first. Growth is change and those in apathetic capital relationship are changing their strategy of how they will do things to succeed in the future.

I used to ride my bike for exercise with a dear friend of mine named Dana. Notice I said the reason for our bike outings was exercise. Dana is an amazing athlete and I was not. So what began as beautiful days biking along the Schuylkill River quickly moved to me being miles behind. In the beginning I was hurt, I wanted to ride along side my friend, but we were out there for a reason - exercise and my initial pace was not exercise for Dana so she had to choose to be about her health business as the top priority. What it did for me after I got past my feelings was challenge me to build up stamina to remain within the vicinity of her pace. My health rapidly improved and so did our relationship. I recognized the importance of staying focused and staying connected. Think about friends who seem to disappear from time to time, what is it they are pursuing while absent? I promise you it is the growth they need to succeed at the next level further down the road.

The hidden beauty I have found in seasons of apathetic capital relationships is that when you bike at your own pace you are setting the pace for others to follow in their own way. Don't stop, keep it moving to the next level of capital relationship — that of the compassionate, we will all be glad you did.

The truth about compassionate capital — a long term relationship of extreme influence

Compassionate capital is at work when there are groups of people successfully investing their talents. Successful models on their own, they choose form alliances around problems worth investing in to solve while remaining independent in their growth areas of opportunity. They are able to see far enough down the road to know how they can support progress for the long term and they do it with what works best for them. Jesus was the master of compassionate capital relationships, he challenged anyone who believed to pick up their bed and walk, to overcome their infirmity and or blindness, to believe that we all are chosen and to work towards bringing heaven on Earth.

It's no secret that I believe in studying and learning from the past. Time spent with our elders allows the past to speak life. I am blessed with mentors who show me what compassionate capital looks like and how to create compassionate relationships. While at my 20th college reunion I ran into one of these mentors, a committed alum of both Hampton and Wharton this man has from the beginning of our relationship held out his hand to guide me further down the road. When I saw him at the reunion I was so happy to chat with him, he had recently retired and was focusing his efforts on strategic investments that would impact future generations. He continued to speak life into my journey and advise me on things to consider along my road. When I left the event I was tired, it had been awesome seeing my old classmates and mentor, it was raining and I wanted to get to my car as quickly as possible. To do that I would have to walk through a dark alley. My mother raised me to never walk through alley ways, always take the main road. Even at 42 I could not betray that order so I to the long route around the buildings, as I crossed the street I got a cramp in my foot and had to grab onto the building in front of me. I began to notice this was a new building on campus, one I had not seen before. Clear as day I heard my inner voice say "look up". As I raised my eyes up the expanse of the building I realized why following my mothers order was the way I am always to go. This new building was named after the mentor I just spoke with! Never did he mention that he had a building constructed on campus, all he said was that he was encouraging the students to research the legacy of the school at the new research center — His research center. At the end of his professional career this man is still building infrastructure to guide future generations to see what he had lived to see.

My prayer is that we all in our own way deploy compassionate capital, for some it will be funding a building, for others it will be writing a book, or speaking to youth who will remember your story and pass it on for generations. Regardless we can all lend a hand in ways our legacy will allow.

What do your community capital relationships look like? What about within your family, amongst your friends, peer groups? What shared desired outcome could you all work towards together? Where can compassionate capital be a reality for you?

Take the time to evaluate which relationships could use a shift in perspective.

Lessons Learned on the NarrowRoad™

The following are questions to help you better understand the NarrowRoad™ you're traveling. Answer as honestly as you can (if you're honest with yourself, your road will narrow to a path conducive to your success). There are no right or wrong answers, even if they don't match everything you've read in this book—remember, for legacy wealth to be attainable, it must be defined by you and the choices you understand.

Question 1: Describe a situation where you have had a sympathetic capital experience

____

____

____

Question 2: Describe a situation where you have had an empathetic capital experience

____

____

____

Question 3: Describe a situation where you have had an apathetic capital experience

____

____

____

Question 4: Describe a situation where you have had a compassionate capital experience

____

____

____

Question 5: What do your community capital relationships look like?

____

____

____

Question 6: Where could you be more compassionate in your financial relationships:

____

____

____

____

Part 5: Our Journey

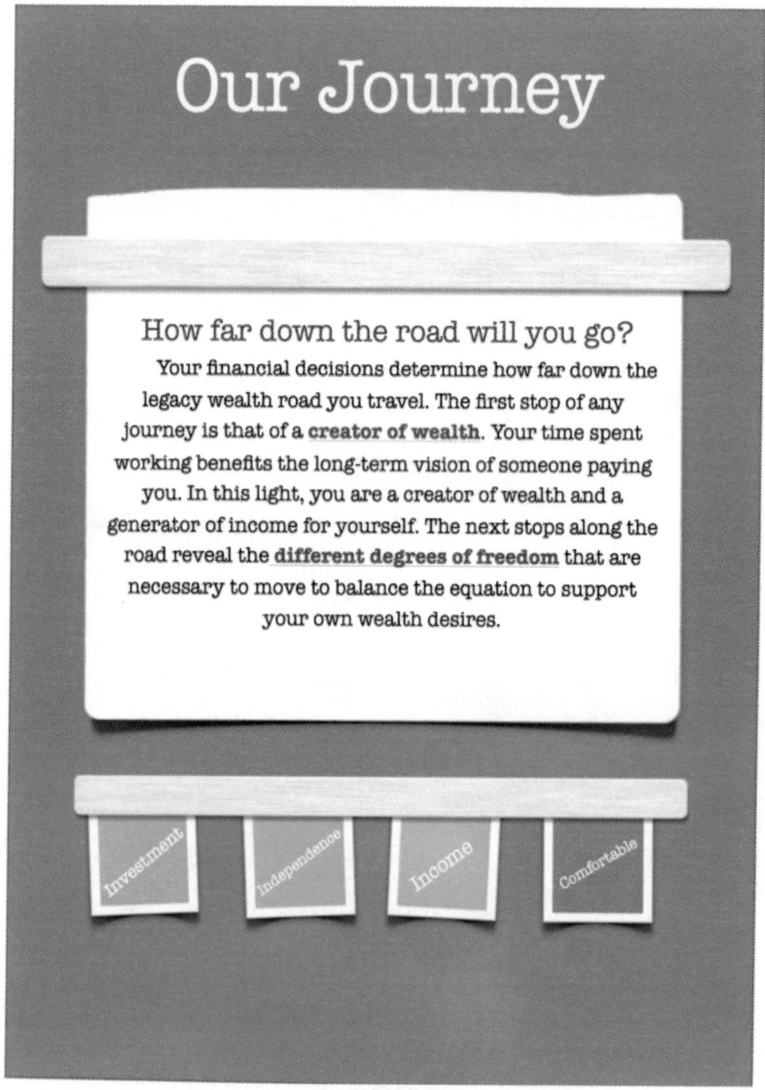

Mynarrowroad.com/journey

Our journey is about picking up the legacy torch and running with it. Nike the goddess of victory and the name of one of the most successful shoe companies had it right. Just do it. Understanding the journey and where you are along the journey helps build momentum. Momentum is what is needed to get further down the road. Collaborations are best when you already have momentum. Designing your pursuit, being confident in your mission is how you build momentum.

Often people would say "just do it, huh?" But do it where? When? How?

Our journey is the blueprint for the how you will get it done. The journey to wealth is how you will apply the concepts you have learned about your unique identity to your possession of promise. Remember in part one we learned history is prophecy if you connect the dots of wisdom knowledge and understanding? Well, the journey to wealth along the NarrowRoad has four steps that occurs individually and collectively at the same time. It occurs individually along your own journey as you must pursue each step your own way. It also occurs collectively as a continuation of a legacy narrative that did not start with you and will not end with you unless you discontinue the conversation. Your journey is a dialog with your past, present and future.

Step One: Creator

Every wealth journey begins with the role of the middleman. The middleman is a term used to describe a journey of owning your way toward success of your choosing. It was penned by Booker T. Washington and is necessary for everyone to master. Income is fuel for the fire of your torch, the seed of your legacy-wealth business. The lesson of work and finding the gift that makes room for you is the key to this first step along the road to wealth.

The Next Step 2—Builder

The next step along the journey to wealth is where things start to get interesting. This is what I call the first degree of freedom. There are degrees of freedom in America, meaning the "99 percent" (ignoring the mega-rich 1 percent of the population) are not all on the same level. The first degree of freedom, "middle-class 101," is often one generation from survival.

With the blessing of consistent income and the use of leverage you can arrive at a sense of comfort. Your lifestyle is beginning to take shape and some of your desires are being met. The lesson of cash-flow is the gauge of the first degree of freedom.

The middle class are what I call "talented." They know how to use leverage, their savings, and their investments to build a life they desire. Learning the requirements of being talented comes best from another torchbearer along the NarrowRoad. His name is W. E. B. Du Bois.

William Edward Burghardt Du Bois (February 23, 1868–August 27, 1963) was an American civil rights activist, leader, Pan-Africanist, sociologist, educator, historian, writer, editor, poet, and scholar. After graduating from Harvard, where he was the first African American to earn a doctorate, he became a professor of history, sociology, and economics at Atlanta University. Du Bois was one of the co-founders of the National Association for the Advancement of Colored People (NAACP) in 1909.

In September 1903 Dr. DuBois wrote an essay titled The Talented Tenth, the essay exposed his beliefs of how his community similar to the plight of other races was to progress further down the road.

"The Negro race, like all races, is going to be saved by its exceptional men. The problem of education, then, among Negroes must first of all deal with the Talented Tenth; it is the problem of developing the Best of this race that they may guide the Mass away from the contamination and death of the Worst, in their own and other races."

Dr. DuBois believed that it would be a group of exceptional men (and, I have to believe, women), educated to lead their community towards the goals that he felt all in his community sought that lived further down the road.

Its technique is a matter for educational experts, but its object is for the vision of seers. If we make money the object of man-training, we shall develop money-makers but not necessarily men; if we make technical skill the object of education, we may possess artisans but not, in nature, men. Men we shall have only as we make manhood the object of the work of the schools–intelligence, broad sympathy, knowledge of the world that was and is, and of the relation of men to it–this is the curriculum of that Higher Education which must underlie true life. On this foundation we may build bread winning, skill of hand and quickness of brain, with never a fear lest the child and man mistake the means of living for the object of life.

As one of the highest academically trained thought leaders in his community, Dr. DuBois realized that it was not knowledge of money alone, nor skill or method that would address the growing problem in his community, rather he knew it was wisdom, knowledge, and understanding, coupled with a compassion and connectedness to each other that was needed for the whole community to move forward towards its promise.

In other words it was not just the talented tenth who were to get ahead, it was also the necessary 90 (as I call them) who were needed for the plan as he saw it to succeed. Wealth is after all a group process.

"If this be true–and who can deny it–three tasks lay before me; first to show from the past that the Talented Tenth as they have risen among American Negroes have been worthy of leadership; secondly to show how these men may be educated and developed; and thirdly to show their relation to the Negro problem."_

In picking up this great mans Torch, I see within his method a similarity to what is needed in rebuilding our communities today. A relationship with the past narratives that can serve as models for the similar problems we face in our own life journeys, a culturally relevant curricula that exposes everyone how to best use their talents, and to elevate the standard of business in community so that we may all look at the problems in our communities as the business opportunities they are. We are all connected, building the life you desire is in part connecting with the group process you have inherited. Using your talents and learning from the talents of others is how you build a life for your self and elevate the standard of business in your community.

"You misjudge us because you do not know us. From the very first it has been the educated and intelligent of the Negro people that have led and elevated the mass..." — W.E.B DuBois

Along the NarrowRoad you will find that black and white don't matter if you understand green. Creating and building a life and communities that we desire requires exchanges of talents and expertise that come from a variety of sources. Build what you desire with the talents in your portfolio and that of others.

Beyond the Lifestyle Journey Is Independence

Learning to balance your present and your future is key to getting further down the road beyond lifestyle on this journey.

Your builder step relies on your ability to exchange with others to build economics of scale for your desire to stabilize your ability to live as you desire. Your builder step requires emotional maturity to establish a better relationship with money first by acknowledging that everyone needs support to be the best they can be. There are many reasons for protest and fighting in the first degree of freedom. Remember that when fighting you will often have very little time and or energy for anything else. As a result to build legacy wealth you must go further down your narrowroad.

The Next Step #3—Grower

The next step along the journey is that of the grower. This step is where you learn how to multiply your talents to grow the capital within your wealth portfolio. This is the second degree of freedom which is a highly productive state of being. You know you have mastered this step when you can afford to do what you want to do and what you desire to do. Growers own the confidence to plant their talents in the various terrains in the financial wilderness and have the time to nurture both.

This second degree of freedom is often three generations from survival. Not only do people in this degree of freedom tend to be middle class, they increase their financial independence by partnering with the middle road. The middle road was a concept created by yet another torchbearer along the NarrowRoad, Kelly Miller. Kelly Miller (1863–1939) if you remember from chapter 6 was a prominent mathematician, sociologist, essayist, newspaper columnist, and author and was the first African American to attend the PhD program at Johns Hopkins. He graduated from Howard University School of Law and as dean of the College of Arts and Sciences; he modernized the old classical curriculum and added new courses in the natural sciences and the social sciences. Kelly Miller was an avid writer and editor who in fact edited Booker T. Washington's and W. E. B.

DuBois's work. He agreed with neither man's work in its entirety, deciding a "middle road" was the best route for the black community to take to freedom. The middle road included both education and vocation, to both study and work using the capitalist system to make a way for his people to move forward.

Kelly Miller's life demonstrates how you can work with perspectives you do not entirely agree with when you have a shared desired outcome. All three men desired for their communities to obtain freedom; when fused, these three legacies create a very compelling system of exchange—first starting with ourselves, our communities, and the world. I find it is as relevant today as it was in Kelly Miller's time.

Your life system supports your purpose, enlightens your big idea, ensures that others understand the strategic advantage you have chosen to get out of the wilderness, helps you win your battles, and focuses your path to take possession of your Promised Land. Step four along the NarrowRoad is where you build such a system for your life, one that speaks life to your unique values and needs for the degree of freedom you desire.

My big idea, when I began this journey, was to build a system of corporately working through narratives of the Bible, beginning with the Promised Land, to pool capital to fund individual and collective pursuits of promise. Pursuits I defined as business systems, capable of engaging various types of people toward a common goal to take possession of. Faith after all was at the center of everything when financial crisis ensued.

When you think about the realities of the costs of retirement we all need a middle road to build wealth in some way. Ownership is the key.

Your grower step relies on your ability to partner with opportunities (e.g., what you are knowledgeable of and confident in pursuing).

The Next Step #4—Expander

The next step along the journey is the role of the expander. This is the step where you are upper middle class this degree of freedom is rare and often four generations from survival. Expanders have traditions and financial rituals that have spanned since they can remember. Expanders can see the value in those journeying behind them and are capable of investing in other people's progress to further expand that of their own legacy.

The requirements of being an expander are revealed in the legacy of yet another torchbearer along the NarrowRoad — Thurgood Marshall. NAACP attorney Thurgood Marshall's dream was to level the playing field. To get to financial emancipation, Thurgood's idea was to plant "seed cases," which in this case were the eleven lawsuits he filed on behalf of African American children in the South and the District of Columbia.

"Five of these cases—from South Carolina; Virginia; Delaware; Washington DC; and Kansas—finally arrived at the Supreme Court in 1952 under the heading of Brown." Marshall had what might seem to be an extremely simple view of the Reconstruction Amendments—the thirteenth, fourteenth, and fifteenth—are designed to secure racial equality.

Your expander step relies on your ability to invest what you see into the lives of others through your number-one quadrant. Expanders create the blueprints that others will both follow and benefit from for generations. Expander leave legacies at show the cultural advantage of getting further down the road together. Everyone can leave a blueprint of the road unseen to most that they have chosen to travel. This enables the blind to see, the confused to learn, momentum to take a quantum leap, and the mute to find their reason to speak. Take the time to find the expander in you, the world needs to benefit from your perspective.

Our Collective Journey

What phase of the journey did you grow up in? Were you raised in a middle-class household? If middle class which degree? Can you see your life journey elevating the standard of legacy to the next degree of freedom? I hope so. Using your NarrowRoad identity and your systems of success you can design a pursuit to take the legacy to the a promise you desire. All you have to do is believe.

Chapter 12: Legacy Wealth Migrations

The pattern of how wealth is created can be well illustrated in the journey from early America to our present day. From the first adventurers who desired to create a better life for themselves in America, who as early pioneers starved to death attempting to make a life working on their own, to the second-generation founders, who joined forces to create the system upon which America quantum-leaped into a position of a superpower, to the Africans whose the transition from slavery to the three degrees of freedom, each example has patterns that resemble that of both the parable of the talents and the hidden treasure in the field. To be the first of anything is a difficult journey that sacrifices much to retain very little. This is evidenced by those groups of people such as the early American settlers predating the Civil War and the emergent sharecroppers post-Emancipation. It is difficult to sustain oneself without an overarching vision for how things should be. It is difficult for first movers to build traction by themselves.

When freedom is offered to a group who are no longer stifled by the ability to use only one talent, how they plan their own life distance between that level of freedom and the first servant level of freedom is matter of ownership in what emancipation provides. Emancipation is defined as the fact or process of being set free from legal, social, or political restrictions; to be liberated. The emancipated slaves had the opportunity to either migrate to another location or sharecrop with former plantation owners and attempt to do what they had done for their former masters for themselves. Resources were limited, and they were beholden to their former masters by borrowing the seed capital required to build some level of freedom for themselves.

The first and second degrees of freedom fall between the sharecropper, who did what they could with what they had, and the migrant who formed networks and groups to work with in uncharted territory. Understanding the various levels of business, how they best operate is very important in overcoming the battles that inherently attack those who are working to make not just a life but a legacy for themselves and others, which includes wealth.

The slavery business model proves to be a very beneficial one for teaching because it has impacted each and every American. Understanding the various journeys enables one to see the different pathways and timeframes that are available to build wealth as you define it. There are many roads that lead to one's ability to impact the future as we will come to know it. All roads that have been taken here in America can enlighten us to what choices and options we cannot afford to wait on pursuing.

It takes three generations to build legacy wealth: one generation to work hard and build a talent (or twenty-plus years of resources), one generation to multiply these talents to form a plan for freedom, and one generation who can grow these talents into a productive system of support for themselves and others. The mastery level is one where anyone with a vision can participate; to be able to see value before it is created is what makes a master capable of reaping harvests where they have not sown seed themselves.

The legacy example of A. G. Gaston (1892–1996), an African American millionaire who learned how to multiply his various talents, was the grandson of sharecroppers. Gaston learned from his grandmother and grandfather, former slaves who worked together post-emancipation as sharecroppers and entrepreneurs. Gaston grew up at a time largely influenced by Booker T. Washington, who encouraged blacks to believe in the philosophy of self-help, racial solidarity, and accommodation. Washington urged blacks to "accept discrimination for the time being and concentrate on elevating themselves through hard work and material prosperity. He believed in education in the crafts, industrial and farming skills, and the cultivation of the virtues of patience, enterprise, and thrift. This, he said, would win the respect of whites and lead to African Americans being fully accepted as citizens and integrated into all strata of society."_

Gaston, after serving in the military, went to work in the mines of Alabama and got the idea to sell lunches to the men he worked with. His mother and grandmother were superior cooks who learned on the plantation. In partnering with her, he was able to establish a business and quite a bit of trust with the men he worked with who then became his customers. This business expanded to lending money at a 25 percent interest and later selling burial insurance to his coworkers, as mining was a dangerous business that often resulted in death. Gaston went on to partner with his father-in-law in the funeral business and later opened a savings bank providing banking services to his community.

Gaston is a perfect example of a second servant who worked with others to fill a need in his extended social network. He grew to that of a first servant as his business endeavors afforded him the opportunity to build enterprises that filled the various needs of his community and proved financially beneficial for those outside of his community. As a legacy he sold his business to his employees, desiring to continue Booker T. Washington's legacy of self-help, hard work, and material prosperity.

Reginald Lewis is an example of how to make a quantum leap from second servant to that of a master. First to attend college in his family, he went on to Harvard Law School. In observing the world of mergers and acquisitions, Lewis quickly saw that the way to wealth creation was through acquisition. Lewis is the first African American to buy a billion-dollar business. In his purchase he opened the doors of employment opportunities to communities that had yet to get beyond the position of the third servant.

There are various ways to build an enterprise capable of sustaining your desired level of freedom. Knowing yourself—your strengths and weaknesses—enables you to engage in a pursuit of multiplying your talents at levels that enable anyone to build wealth however they define it.

In the case of African Americans, their first entrance into the American business model was not as an agent but as capital or goods to be used as an input to build a colony into a global superpower. The labor of those first movers enabled the initial harvest that funded the start-up operations of the migrators, who then used the returns to fuel the engine required for America to break free from European rule.

We are all different types of servants in different types of situations, and each situation has its own gold in the land. My grandmother said, "The only thing God is not making any more of is time and land, so steward both wisely." Wise stewardship is what action is all about when it comes to transitioning from that of a creator of wealth to a wealth creator for yourself. For anyone to become a master, he or she must be a servant; this is true in all things. It is through giving that one prepares to receive. The understanding of business makes the giving and receiving equitable, allowing both parties to value the exchange in whatever currencies they desire. Slavery can remain a thing of the past when you learn how to exchange and operate your talents in your field of dreams and opportunities.

Why does this matter? The lesson is to look not to the left or the right but acknowledge the independent pursuit within you and steward your time wisely. Recognize the mastery level of those who came before you. Shifting your perspective in this way will provide opportunity and reward you for your time as you focus on the business development of yourself and others. Sometimes you have to work different parts of you field to uncover your hidden treasure buried within you.

Summary of the Servant Levels and Talents

- ☐ **Talent one**: cultural capital
- ☐ **Talent two**: intellectual capital
- ☐ **Talent three**: human capital—people create knowledge, new ideas, and new products, and they establish relationships that make processes truly work. Unfortunately, when people leave, they take along their knowledge, including internal, external, formal, and informal relationships.
- ☐ **Talent four**: social capital
- ☐ **Talent five**: spiritual capital
- ☐ **First servant**: pools all five talents into a system that grows value everywhere they journey
- ☐ **Second servant**: exchanges weaknesses (talent 4) for strengths (talent 3) and builds collaborations to utilize obtain access to up to four talents (talent 2 and talent 1)
- ☐ **Third servant**: does all the work initially with his third talent (human capital); is successful in the short term but struggles delivering results when working alone

I have spoken with thousands of individuals, many of them clients. The patterns I observe never cease to amaze me. They are patterns that can be traced back to the Israelites wandering in the wilderness and followed into our more recent history. The most prevalent patterns can be seen in our parents and grandparents. Here I will share a couple of examples of the mistakes many of us are making. These are the simple mistakes that could be the difference between achieving second or third servant level instead of mastery. Some of these brief overviews illustrate some patterns that may seem familiar to you.

Angela and Troy owned three businesses and multiple homes together but somehow were often short on cash. They were young, newly married, and making moves to generate as much income as they could and couldn't understand why they still struggled at times. Their response to lack was to start more money-making efforts.

While working with them, I asked them how far in the future they looked to determine their level of financial health. Were they building a legacy that would lead to wealth? When examining their timescale, they realized that while they were accumulating assets and owning businesses, they were emergent-minded and committed to "now." They had not yet learned how to look beyond their income to find their legacy.

So we created a "now" budget, and it revealed there was no thinking or planning around their cash flow, the inflows and outflows of money, so when it came in, it also went out. To cover their cash-flow shortages, they turned to debt, further impacting their cash flow and eventually ruining their credit.

It's a problem when we don't understand who we are in relation to the flow of our money. Money which is really just our time—human capital multiplied by an hourly or annual wage. Without this understanding, we loose sight of how to balance the needs of ourselves and others, and in the moment often we are not able to react in ways that build, grow, and expand our opportunities. When faced with financial challenges, the fastest way to get hustled is to be on the hustle and not aware of one's most vulnerable currency. You must value what you have, really all that you have, in order to value other people and understand the connection they have to building your lifestyle and your reality. Typically, the way we "do" one thing is also the way we "do" everything. This "do" behavior maps what we value most and leads to a greater understanding to our style of exchange.

After working with the couple to help them shift their perspective further down the road toward legacy, they were able to see that positive cash flow was required to elevate their standard of business beyond that of survival. They promptly sold one of their properties, paid off some debt, started a to seriously save and manage their spending to a level that was within their means. Once the picture they were posing for was framed they were able to change their pose accordingly.

Perception versus Reality

Stacy had run her own business for nearly fifteen years. She was well-known, liked, respected … and barely making it. On the outside, she looked like a mover and shaker and had received many awards for the impact she was making in her community. But on the inside, she was struggling to make ends meet and bitterly aware of the contradiction between perception and reality. She came up to me after a speaking engagement and said, "I need to talk to you. I make too much money to not have any."

She needed financing to sustain and expand to a competitive scale, but her accounting books were suspect because she used her company as an "ATM," so no bank would lend to her. She had tried and failed to find a partner to secure the added resources, but she'd been going it alone for so long that she couldn't concede anything, making it nearly impossible to partner, co-build, or align with anyone.

On the surface, Stacy was a small businesswoman—resourceful, passionate, committed, capable—but inside she was stuck because her understanding of money and her relationship with it was so limited. But there was more to it than that. Because she was so financially illiterate, she was always insecure and at a loss when money was involved and terrified of being "hustled." That mistrust of herself translated into a mistrust of others and ultimately resulted in her inability to pick the right partners and make good deals. Stacey's fear made her unaware of what she did not know.

Her financial and business illiteracy was partnered with a level of financial oppression that spanned for generations. She felt shame from the reality that she had squandered her inheritance from both sides of the family trying to look the part she had no clue how to master. While she grew up in a grower family, attended the right schools, and made the right connections, she had not a clue how to expand it to the next level. But she did know what it looked like, and so the surface of appearances continued.

We worked together on growing her understanding of money so that she could interact with others from a place of confidence. She learned how to first identify and then face her fears on a consistent basis, this unlocked her voice to ask for the real help she needed and continue on her personal journey to her promise. Stacy is now cash-flow positive and growing quite nicely. She is enjoying having a team on her side to work with and a bank that wants her to succeed as much as she does.

It's Personal When It Should Be Business

He was an established pastor who came from a long line of ministers. He grew up in a home that was nothing like the one he had created with his ministry. People traveled far and wide to attend his church. He had the heart of a father who wanted what he did not have growing up for those who attended his church. The congregation looked to him for guidance and support in everything, including finances. He desired to provide the support they needed as a ministry within the church. Yet financial and business literacy and knowledge of how to raise the capital to build in this area of ministry did not presently live within the church leadership or congregation. Together they were wandering in the wilderness looking for someone to unearth their treasure.

The support they needed required a different level of business than the pastor and his leadership were accustomed to. It required changes in the core of how they operated, namely working with a shared vision that lived outside the day-to-day operations of the church and its ministry. This had to include the financial regulations of systems in society, namely banking and insurance. It was clear that both financial and business acumen were needed to support such a dream. The pastor was often approached by people desiring to be of service to him and his congregation. Not quite confident himself of the fundamentals of personal finance, home and business ownership, he was not in a position to screen those who wanted to support his dream of assisting his congregation. He had not the eyes to protect both his own and his congregational vulnerabilities. He had the right intentions but the wrong level of emotional maturity to admit he was out of his degree of freedom.

The company that was brought in to advise the congregation was a small business with hidden agendas. The pastor was not able to recognize these hidden elements, and as a result, many of the members were either ill advised or lost their homes and most of their retirement savings by investing in opportunities that were not in their best interest. Sadly, talents buried in the sand were taken away due to misinformation, miseducation and fear of going to people with a track record of advising clients, namely local and national banks in the area.

When I met this pastor, he was shamed and depressed at how such a good intention could go so wrong. My belief is that when navigating uncharted territory, we need an expert who is adept, proven, and regulated, a master at the craft we are unsure of. Our personal relationships with what could be well intentioned but emergent businesses are not the way to lead those vulnerable to wealth creation. Helping the pastor to see this was the first step in a long road to healing broken relationships and devastated believers desiring to arrive at their Promised Land.

Lessons Learned along the NarrowRoad

The following will help you better understand the NarrowRoad you're traveling. Answer as honestly as you can (if you're honest with yourself, your road will narrow to a path conducive to your success). There are no right or wrong answers, even if they don't match everything you've read in this book—remember, for legacy wealth to be attainable, it must be defined by you and the choices you understand.

1: Describe the freedoms you feel you have in your present life experiences:

____

____

____

2: Describe the road you have selected to migrate to improve your current situation:

____

____

____

3: Describe the migration you are presently pursuing:

____

____

____

4: How far down the road do you intend to travel with the business of you—freedom, growth, or expansion?

____

____

____

5: What areas do you need help with to get to the next degree of freedom?

____

____

____

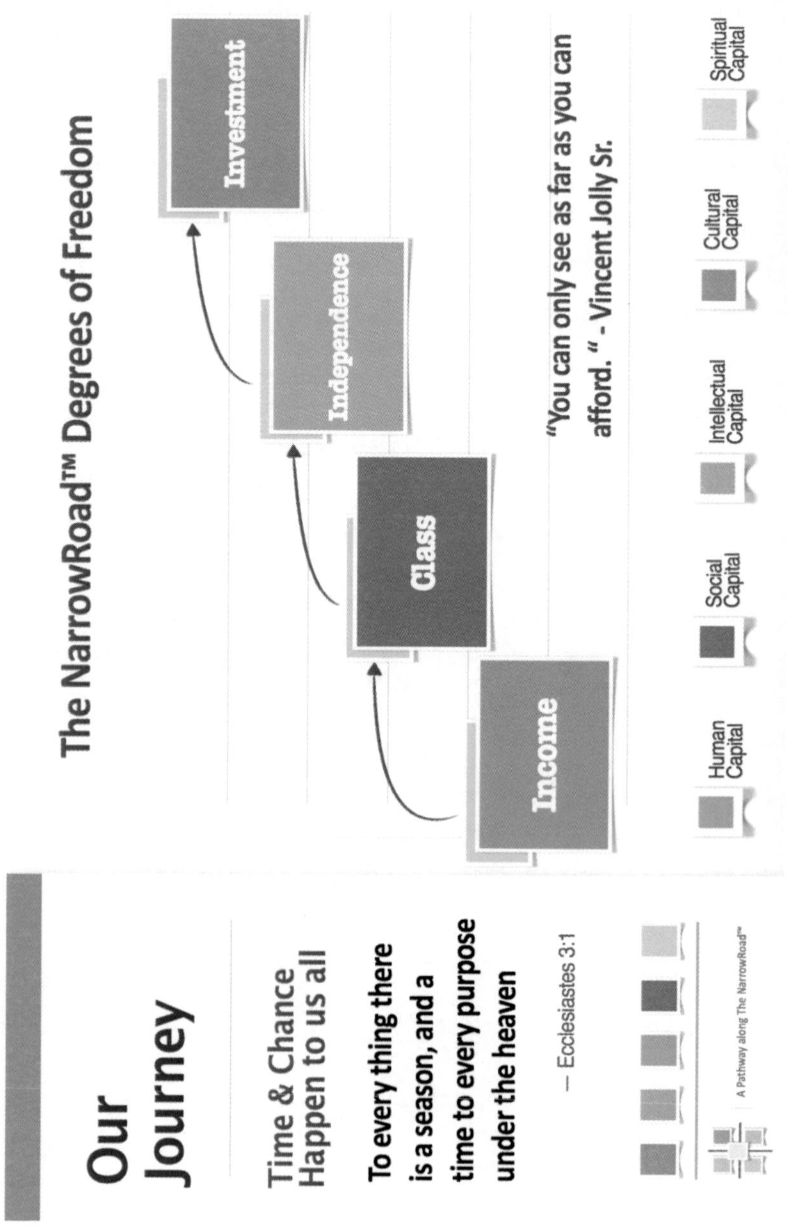
Our Journey
Time & Chance Happen to us all
To every thing there is a season, and a time to every purpose under the heaven
— Ecclesiastes 3:1
A Pathway along The NarrowRoad™
The NarrowRoad™ Degrees of Freedom
Income
Class
Independence
Investment
"You can only see as far as you can afford." - Vincent Jolly Sr.
Human Capital
Social Capital
Intellectual Capital
Cultural Capital
Spiritual Capital

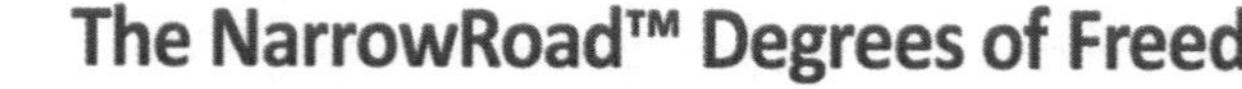

Chapter 13: Your NarrowRoad Journey

There is nothing new under the sun. The race is not to the swift, nor the battle to the strong, neither yet bread to the wise, nor yet riches to men of understanding, nor yet favor to women of skill; but time and chance happen to them all.

— Ecclesiastes 9:11(KJV)

A roadmap offers a step-by-step process to chart a path to reach your desired outcome. Strategy and structure are you partners for wealth creation your way. The first objective of the NarrowRoad is to co-create a life business system to get where you desire most to go —beyond the financial wilderness. The method to build this roadmap is a narrative survey which consists of a series of questions that when answered and reflected upon through the lens of your NRID, began a journey from where you presently are in the wilderness to the next degree of freedom you desire to go.

- ☐ Entry gate—Finding my NarrowRoad ID.
- ☐ Assessment—Where in the wilderness am I?
- ☐ Wealth checklist—Where are the blind spots along my road?
- ☐ Inquiry—What is my strategy to define and own where I want to go from here?
- ☐ Convincing—What must I do? (Now, next, ongoing, long-term)
- ☐ Persuasion—What must I ask for from my wealth team and demand of myself?
- ☐ Negotiation—How far down the road must I look to get where I desire to go? What must I face to get beyond my roadblock?

Wealth is a group process—individuals journeying together in a collective pursuit. With the right group you can stay on task.

A Personalized Roadmap beyond the Pitfalls

Your life is what you make of it. You are a servant with the potential of five talents capable of planting seeds, and reaping harvests. Your life is yours to design how you see fit—when viewed this way it truly is a gift.

Regardless of where you begin, where you end is entirely up to you and your choices. The road is the same for everyone what is different is your unique perspective. Think of your perspective as a window with five panes. Your journey is the frame.

The NarrowRoad system distills your many options into a few explicit choices. Your choices custom the NarrowRoad roadmap beginning where you are currently positioned in the financial wilderness, helping you to detail what you desire to build, grow, and expand, and ending at your ultimate desired outcome.

A step-by-step process to chart a path to reach your desired outcome

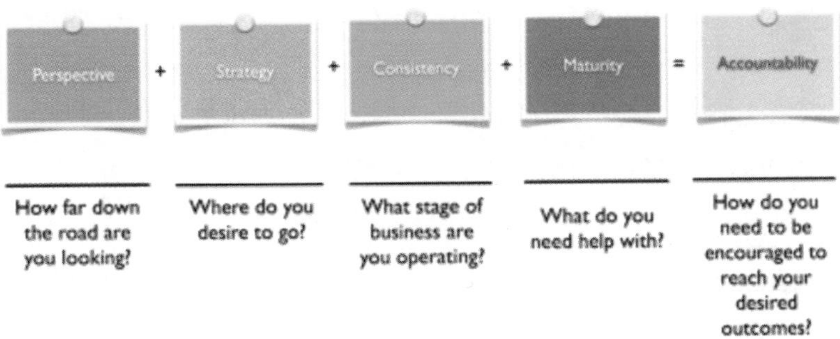

These are the steps along the NarrowRoad that get you where you desire to go. Perspective is shaped by your history, your experiences, your confidence, and your vulnerabilities. Where have you come from as an individual, as a member of society, as a leader of your own pursuit of promise? How far back down the road have you taken the time to look? What is the history you have already created? Writing your story leads to writing your vision. Making it plan is how you go deeper with the assistance of your NRID. Waiting for it is how you operate the business of you. Seeing it come to pass is how you actualize your legacy.

Strategy is at the root of your confidence, the use of applied knowledge that will weather any storm in your life, downturn in the market, and disappointment in your point of view. Are you confident you are pursuing wealth with the right strategy? Financial growth is really about partnering with a level of financial independence you believe is right for you. Each level has fundamental steps needed to grow this level of independence. For instance, the level of financial independence you desire post-retirement narrows the road to a few select strategies to save and invest for it. College for your children is similar in this way. Learn the fundamentals, and your strategy for financial independence takes shape.

Consistency is the key to fruitful outcomes. Anything will work if you work it. Anything. I used to buy all this workout equipment and would soon grow tired of it, and I would tell anyone who would listen that the equipment simply did not work. My trainer would say, "If you worked it, it would work just as promised. You gave up—it didn't."

Consistency is key to moving further down the road closer to the authentic you. Where in your life are you most consistent? Where are you the least consistent? Why is this? Belief drives action. The NarrowRoad roadmap will work if you work it. Your NarrowRoad ID will tell us what needs to be reinforced in your strategy so that consistency is a choice you commit to.

Maturity—to arrive at a state of consistency requires taking a look at your beliefs in the areas your consistency needs assistance. Maturity is how we get where we desire to go. Our relationship with money can be very emotional. It's time to face our deepest fears about the desires of our hearts. Life is a scary place when you avoid facing what matters most. You find yourself alone, faking it till you make it. How mature are your emotions? In matters of the heart and wealth, one must play to both their strengths and weaknesses to build a life they desire. How mature are you really when it comes to what you desire most? What must you face to get beyond where you are most comfortable?

Who holds you accountable for your ideas and dreams encased in your perspective? Remaining consistent, staying true to your strategy, getting mature all requires accountability. As we get older, accountability partners are optional—you will find they need to be a staple in your life-purpose pursuit. An accountability network is key; wealth is, after all, a group process.

In this chapter, our journey will explore the system of the NarrowRoad. Systems are neutral; it is people who are biased. You bias the NarrowRoad system with your NarrowRoad ID (NRID). The answers to the key questions reveal what is true to you. The system reveals a narrative based on your answers that when understood guides you further down the road to the life you most desire.

In talking with thousands of people, there are patterns of pain points where everyone in some way gets stuck. A pain point is a condition of "stuckness" between where you are now and where you want to be. The pain can be physical suffering, mental and or emotional discomfort that can last over a prolonged period of time.

There are pain points throughout the various terrains in the wilderness. As we learned earlier, there are four terrains in the financial wilderness. Each terrain has valuable lessons that, once learned, fortify our journey so that we can move beyond stuckness to what we desire most.

Which area of the wilderness are you currently navigating?

- ☐ **Rocky**—rejections that protect you from losing what matters most
- ☐ **Thorny**—challenges that strip away the fluff
- ☐ **Fertile**—sweet spots where you can do nothing but win
- ☐ **Landmines**—triggers that upset the best-laid plans

This is where we begin your personal roadmap. The objective of the NarrowRoadmap is to provide clarity about your path along the NarrowRoad. This consists of:

- ❑ A clear understanding of the business of you
- ❑ A custom strategy to get out of the financial wilderness that you understand
- ❑ A system that meets you where you are and guides you to where you desire most to go

The NarrowRoad meets you where you are—your current situation. This is our starting point. However far down the road you want to look is where you begin today. For some it is the distance between today and tomorrow, or between now and next month, for others is the distance between now and the next promotion or retirement. Given the time value of money, now is the best time you will ever have to start your journey to legacy wealth. You do need a guide to ensure you avoid the common pitfalls one faces while attempting to get out of the financial wilderness.

Compound interest allows anyone to sow a seed and reap a harvest. Unconsciously we make investments in other people's legacy wealth plan, so why not do the same for yourself? The patented component of the NarrowRoad is what makes this system unique. The first step is to get to know yourself on a deeper, more vulnerable level—your self-worth and value. You are your first business; trust that, and you will change your whole outlook.

Getting beyond a Pain Point

Become literate. Every step along the NarrowRoad has an operating system. Systems have languages. Determine what the key words are and how you define them. If you don't know the words you cannot build the wealth.

- ☐ Manage your interpretation — How can these terms be used to address your intended outcome?
- ☐ Invest your perspective to assign a cultural meaning. Ask yourself, in light of how I view things, what is most meaningful to me?
- ☐ Risk rejection with the truth of your belief — reject the business as usual in our community
- ☐ Anchor your focus to a milestone further down the road
- ☐ Get beyond the storm and recognize what financial stewardship of your talents really means
- ☐ Get to a growth mode where you are confident enough to partner with others
- ☐ Get beyond yourself to a legacy where you can invest your time, talent, and treasure in future generations.

It takes three generations to build legacy wealth and only one generation to lose it. Don't start from scratch. Take the time to dig for hidden treasure. There is value in connection, so let's build wealth together.

So you want to know what stands in the way of your next degree of freedom? The most insistent pinpoint lives in your fourth quadrant, the place where you are most vulnerable financially. Armed with your NarrowRoad ID, you will be able to face your fears about pursuing the level of financial independence you desire.

What Is My Current Strategy? Lifestyle or Legacy?

Your initial strategy is a seed that over time will create the financial independence you need. Everyone needs financial independence to feel confident about their future. A confident mind makes the shrewdest decisions. It is an insecure mind that cannot learn. Learning is a large part of strategy because strategies navigate the changes that are inevitable to occur over your lifetime. If you have a strategy, you are playing to your advantage. Advantage is where the fun begins.

I was a strategist at a company called Accenture, and one of the wonderful things I loved the most was the ability to take a problem, a question, or a current situation and form a proposed solution that stimulated the deepest desires of the company while exposing the most vulnerable weaknesses of the people desiring to build the company stronger. The ability to think through the issues, opportunities, supporting data, and systems needed to connect these dots curled my toes. Learning from that experience gave me the insight into why communities I cared about would start with a great idea and fizzle in the early stages of development and spend the rest of their time working hard to make it work with limited resources. You need a team to make the idea a dream, and the first member of that team should be a strategist.

The NarrowRoad helps you formulate the critical elements together to get to a strategy that when executed yields the maximum advantage. Along the road you will be introduced to experts who will teach you the fundamentals so that your choices are informed.

So what is the next step you want to take toward legacy wealth? We call this your first degree of freedom. (Degrees of freedom is a statistical term that refers to the number of values in the final calculation of a statistic that are free to vary. In other words, the degree of freedom can be defined as the minimum number of independent coordinates that can completely specify the position of the system.)

Along the NarrowRoad, there are three degrees of freedom: building, growth, and expansion. These are the three strategies that one takes along the NarrowRoad.

What must be bridged together to get there? A strategy that is executed connects the dots between where you are to where you desire to go. It marks the steps into a roadmap for you to pursue confidently. This mean you understand the value of each step to your life purpose, which includes the lifestyle and legacy perspectives.

Convincing—What Must I Do Right Now?

Your mission is to operate your life in ways that align with your now established legacy perspective. The field is vast with opportunity. The seed, which is the strategy you plant, is up to you. Your mission is to work the ground around your seed so that it survives the time it needs in the area of the field you have planted in. Look at your life. What part of the field are you spending time in? What area of your personal business must you focus on to move forward?

Persuasion—What Must I Ask For?

Everyone in the wilderness needs help getting out. Everyone needs help bringing the full crop to harvest. Everyone. Wealth is a group process. Without a group, wealth is a nice topic, but who will you discuss it with? Without connections and relationships, how will you pass on your legacy? It is for these reasons that not going it alone is the key to the various degrees of freedom.

The first degree of freedom is the ability to build with others. To form groups of like-minded individuals and hearts that either want what you want or want you to get what you want. Do you have these groups in your possession of capital? This is your social capital. Your social capital is not your thousand-plus friendships on Facebook, LinkedIn or Twitter. That is your alliance capital. Social capital and alliance capital is different. Alliance capital are others with whom you both share an appreciation to observe each other's lives for inspiration and development. Social capital is based on the ability to exchange wants for needs to arrive at the desires of your heart.

Many of us misuse or misunderstand social capital. We simply don't know how to use the power of a great group. Great groups have been known to come together for a single purpose and by exchanging their strengths for their weaknesses they build something amazing. If you look at the game changers in our world they were created not by an individual but a great group. Some great examples of social capital exchanges that build degrees of freedom include:

The story of Berkshire Hathaway—a visionary who initially partnered with friends and family turned investors to build long term wealth

The legacy of Reginald Lewis—a thinker who, through the acquisition in 1987 of the Beatrice

Companies, quantum leaped to wealth creation via ownership

The narrative of the movie industry—which tells the story of early Hollywood and how, in the midst of rejection, Jews created an Empire of their own

The story of hip-hop— a movement that transitioned from music to a way of life

The journey of Asian community to parity—which reveals how a minority group arrives at entrepreneurial parity in eighteen years through closed looped economic circles that anchor in every city and span generations.

Your Weaknesses Are Really Strengths

Your journey thus far along the NarrowRoad has revealed that you have unique external and internal qualities that allow you to create, build, grow, and expand legacy wealth using the talents we have within us. One of my favorite philosophers is Jean Piaget, an extensive researcher who devoted a considerable amount of time to understanding the human process of knowing. Piaget determined that "all of us bring our own particular abilities and dispositions to organize, interact with, and make sense out of the objective world." At each stage of our development we have a particular mental system for organizing thought and behavior to adapt to the environment. This capacity is what Piaget calls one's "psychological structure. The structure is grounded in our innate tendency to organize reality into a coherent system, and it systematizes reality into a manageable enterprise."

Accommodation, Assimilation, and Equilibrium

Your life is a series of interactions between you and reality. Piaget claimed "there are two complementary aspects to this interaction: assimilation and accommodation."

Assimilation is the process by which you define your reality; individual to you, it is how you come into relationship with your present situation in your own way.

Accommodation, on the other hand, is the activity by which the structure of your life is modified and changed in response to incoming data from your present environment.

In other words, your ability to process data is not just based on your own terms. Those terms are in some way altered by data from reality, outside influences, and the way they make you feel. A situation can in this way influence a person's confidence level, and it shifts or changes their structure of living in some way.

"The filtering or modification of incoming information is called assimilation; the modification of internal life systems to fit reality is called accommodation. These twin activities of the unique life system enables a person to adapt to the environment." The balancing of the processes of assimilation and accommodation is what Piaget calls adaptation. From the interaction of the two, a person adapts to the environment to maintain equilibrium.

Piaget goes on to explain that the "activity of equilibrium" has characteristics:

- ☐ Stability—a steady state of living
- ☐ Change or external intrusion to modify it
- ☐ Active engagement—the greater the equilibrium, the more activity is required.
- ☐ Self-regulation—if equilibrium is to be maintained, it requires a constant self-regulating activity.

Freedom is a balancing act of accommodation and assimilation, a give and take from your present reality to define your world. The constant conversation one has with himself and the world when seeking equilibrium is what "gives rise to the ongoing development of a person's ability to know the world."

As one progresses through life's genesis, exodus, wilderness, battles, and ultimately Promise, the "ongoing interaction of a person with the world, in the quest for equilibrium and balance between internal and external factors causes the cognitive structures to develop so that the person becomes more capable of knowing the world at higher levels of cognition."

When you are pursuing the Promise, you are really pursuing a life of purpose. Maslow calls it self-actualization, Piaget calls it shared praxis, and Jung calls it persona. The pursuit of purpose strengthens the very area in which you feel you are the weakest.

However, surrendering the preconceived weakness can be a daunting job. It calls for a person to face his or her insecurities and to uncover and analyze the source of it. In many cases, these insecurities are preconceived weaknesses as a result of an incident during our upbringing. Once we face that thing we've been hiding from, it loses its power and dissolves into the nothingness from whence it came. The gates are open, and we are able to speak the messages contained in our truth, and freedom is now capable of navigating its varying levels defined by you.

It is within your pursuit of purpose that lies your moment of truth. The void that you must balance in the act of surrendering of perceived weaknesses with the belief in a power greater than yourself. A power that knew you before you formed in your mother's womb, and knew that every experience, every choice, every idea was preparing you to be exactly what is needed today to arrive at your life Promise. Surrender is an advanced level of commitment. This commitment is enlightened by understanding your life system which carries a unique level of accuracy for you. Along the NarrowRoad one is taught to become more accountable to desires of your heart and the pursuit of freedom in having them.

Whenever you avoid engaging in your life's purpose, you mute your voice. Your life takes on a mask where it can appear to be the life you dream of, but the truth lies underneath. Similar to a life lived on the surface, you hide from your truth, and when fear comes in, you run from it, the very thing you desire most. Appearances often cover your deepest voids, the dark places that exist between the degrees of freedom regulated by the boundaries one sets between their relationship with the life they have and the life they most desire to have.

The purpose of your life is fueled by the fire of what you feel. When your voice is muted, your message is not being heard and nurtured. When it is not nurtured it is limited, hidden, like talents buried in the sand, hidden treasure in your field, left for others to accidentally find. A life out of sync with its purpose can cause one to become confused, blind, stuck, and/or muted. The fourth step along your NarrowRoad is your life agreement with what lies deepest in your heart, it is what matters most. When it is not connected to your values, your life can begin to speak the messages of outside influences.

A life that speaks your truth has your meaning; it is authentic. Your life demonstrates a reason for living. There is an interconnected purpose to your actions, thoughts, emotions, and ideas, and this fuels your ability to see clearly and think confidently about the promises you desire to pursue.

The Language of Promise

On the last leg of the journey to taking possession of the Promised Land, each tribe had to build a degree of freedom according to their own standard of desired living. Gone were the days where the tribes lived under the standards of the wilderness, where manna and quail, fire and clouds were visible daily to guide their way. Their final assignment was to take full possession and build from the old corn of the land, which is the current resources available as found in Joshua 5:11.

Israel received all the land God had sworn to give to their fathers. As they took possession of it and settled in, God gave them rest on every front, just as He had sworn to their fathers. Not one of their enemies remained facing them. God gave them power over all their enemies. Not one promise of all the good promises that God spoke to the house of Israel remained unfulfilled. We find this in Joshua 21:43–45: everything came true; however, it took generations to get there.

Negotiation—How Far down the Road Must I Look?

With the right group, a dimension of Promise can be harvested. Your choice of lifestyle or legacy is determined by how far down the road you are looking. The reality of great groups is that many of them have a time limit. Some groups are able to last for a few seasons, and some groups are to arrive at a desired outcome in the near term. Some groups are able to accomplish a specific target goal. Few are able to transition what makes them great to the next generation. It is for this reason succession is an important part of wealth building. Each generation has their idea of greatness; to succeed great works to the next generation, the vision must be expanded to include a different and younger perspective, one that has not had the purview of the road you have traveled to get to where you are. They have not executed your strategy or mission assignments, lived in your purpose, or been driven by the insights that trigger your ideas and dreams. The only ones with the front seat to that perspective are you and those closest to you, often your peers.

So how far down the road you are looking determines the length of your harvest. Is it to sustain your pursuit? More than 85 percent of all businesses serve the sole purpose of sustaining the lifestyle of the owner. Or is your focus to expand beyond you? Do you desire to invest in the current realities of those coming after you? This is the negotiation you must consider when taking full ownership of your dream.

Assumed leadership is much different from succeeded leadership. Assumed leadership is when someone comes behind and does not necessarily pick up where you left off. They often reorganize the design that has worked with little understanding of the signs, symbols, and miracles that made the success possible in the first place. This type of assumed leadership leaves a lot of equity under the table. Hidden like potential yet to be inherited.

Learning how to negotiate is the key to expansion while you are living. We are all individuals journeying the same road with similar outcomes and independent strategies based on our unique needs, wants, and missions. How does that align into one vision?

This is the source of most blind spots. How do I negotiate my perspective with the desires of others? You must first be enlightened and learn how to negotiate. The vision after all is for an appointed time and thou it tarry it will eventually come to pass. Some of it may have to be succeeded to the next generation for you to see it. How far down the road are you looking? It is all about you or the legacy of how you have designed your abundant living. Will you take the time to write your legacy narrative so that others will be able to receive the fullness of the torch your passing. Or will vital parts of it be lost in translation and an inability to negotiate. The choice again is up to you.

Wealth is a group process of individuals journeying in a collective pursuit of desired outcomes that are similar but not the same.

Wealth is often explained in parables, stories with hidden multidimensional meanings that are translated by a cultural worldview.

Wealth is a series of exchanges and collaborations based on individuals valuations.

Wealth requires a group agreement that build trust and structure over time.

Chapter 14: Lessons Learned on the NarrowRoad

Reviewing your NarrowRoad Journey

Chapter 12 highlights the steps along the NarrowRoad you have learned and presents a roadmap to what is still needed to accomplish the confidence to build legacy wealth. Answering the questions: Where do we go from here? What must we ask from our wealth team? How far down the road must we look to get where we desire to go? These questions further guide you to the path custom tailored for you.

The following are questions to help you better understand the NarrowRoad you're traveling. Answer as honestly as you can (if you're honest with yourself, your road will narrow to a path conducive to your success). There are no right or wrong answers, even if they don't match everything you've read in this book—remember, for legacy wealth to be attainable, it must be defined by you and the choices you understand.

Question 1: Considering your visionary type, how far down the road are you looking?

____

____

____

Question 2: Considering your thinker type, describe what is needed to feel the most confident about where you desire to go.

____

____

____

Question 3: Considering your current financial situation, what level of business are you currently operating?

____

____

____

Question 4: Considering your speaker type, what do you need help with to succeed at your desired degree of freedom?

____

____

____

Question 5: Considering your desired level of promise, what do you need most to hold you accountable to reach it?

____

____

____

Legacy is more than money. Remember the roles you play in your life as you answer these questions. Remember, your pursuit can teach future generations.

Creating the NarrowRoad has been for me a journey of purpose. The pursuit of promise is a bend in the road, and I am following my mother's advice: I am not ending, I am turning a corner and pursuing the dimension of promise. Join the journey with me, and let's go far together. The specifics of what the Promised Land is entirely up to you. Once the Israelites took possession of the Promised Land, the real fun began—building wealth together.

`I have created programs and workshops for the following segments of our community based on my research and client experiences.

- ☐ Men—www.mynarrowroad.com/men
- ☐ Women—www.mynarrowroad.com/women
- ☐ Businesses—www.mynarrowroad.com/businesses
- ☐ Pastors—www.mynarrowroad.com/pastors
- ☐ Professionals—www.mynarrowroad.com/professionals
- ☐ Youth—www.mynarrowroad.com/youth

I hope you join the journey. There are several ways to do that.

- ☐ Join the NarrowRoad newsletter
- ☐ Come to an event in a city near you
- ☐ Take a module to explore a specific dimension of your wealth strategy
- ☐ Journal the journey with me for a year
- ☐ Join/help me create a legacy wealth group with interest similar to you
- ☐ All of the above

These offers will pop up throughout the year. Ignite your flame with a torch to be made aware of offers that are most interesting to you. Lastly this journey for me is life long. I am committed to reaching the Promised Land (how ever you define it) with those who desire to in my lifetime. It begins with you and understanding your wealth identity. So enter the gate of the NarrowRoad and chart a path towards the next desired outcome best for you. You and your legacy will be glad you do.

Stay blessed.

Part 6: Our Business

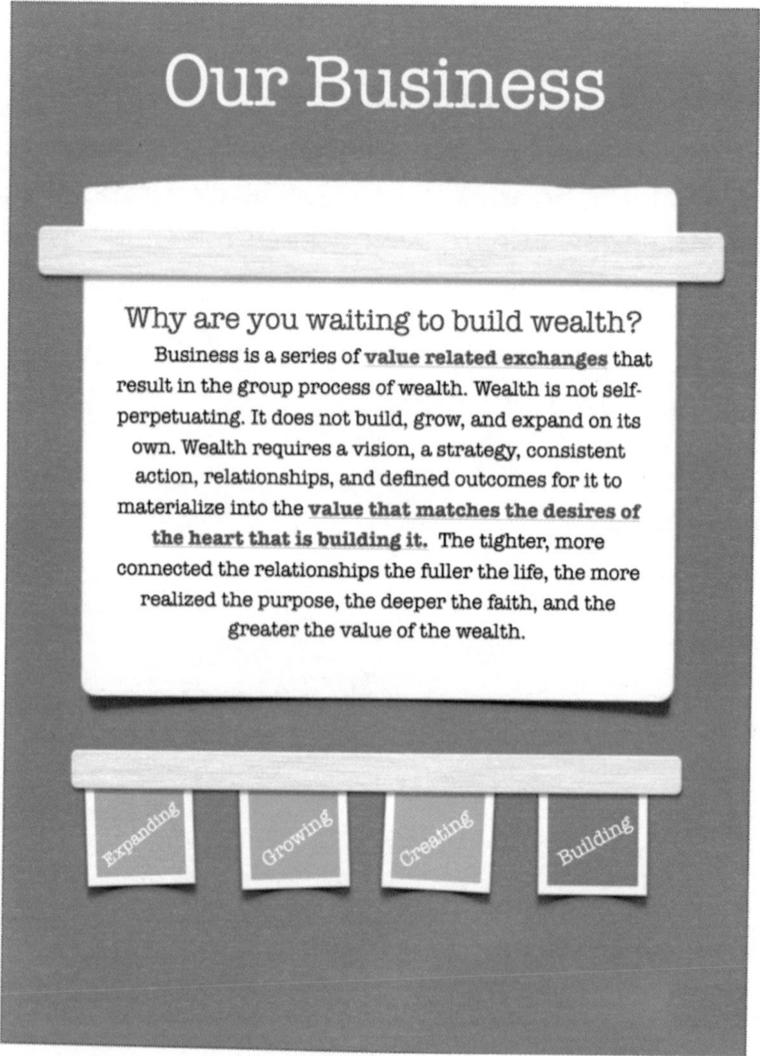

Business is a series of value related exchanges that result in the group process of wealth.

Chapter 15: Why We Are Waiting

There is nothing new under the sun. The race is not to the swift, nor the battle to the strong, neither yet bread to the wise, nor yet riches to men of understanding, nor yet favor to women of skill; but time and chance happen to them all.

— Ecclesiastes 9:11(KJV)

The Reverend Dr. Martin Luther King Jr. posited a question that still remains critical for today: Where do we go from here? He gave us two options to choose from—community or chaos. Which are you choosing? Chaos is disorder, disarray, disorganization, confusion, mayhem, havoc, turmoil, tumult, commotion, disruption, upheaval, uproar. These are part of our daily conversation in today's economy. Community, on the other hand, is a feeling of fellowship with others as a result of sharing common attitudes, interests, and goals. Where is community present in your legacy narrative?

How does your community support your desire to build legacy wealth?

Many of us, I have found along my Jolly-journey, are struggling with an internal battle with our relationships with money, the past, the present, and our future. Notice I said a battle, not a war. The war on wealth has been won for American. Our nation's history, legacy, pursuit, roadmap, journey, and business all have proven that we (as a nation) are wealth-builders. The battle becomes, how do you pick up the torch of that legacy for yourself? How do you make it your reality?

I once read a study that said 4 percent of us are leaders and 96 percent are followers. If that is true, you need to either pick up the torch and lead others in your community toward legacy wealth or follow someone who is holding the torch in front of you. Regardless, one of the these options is necessary for us all to get to the Promised Land together. My grandfather said to me, "In life there are always going to be many options, but there really is only one choice that is right for you, so choose wisely." Please follow the sage advice of Alphonse Jolly, Sr. It worked for him and it can work for you.

The title of this chapter is in response to Dr. King's question. In my research I found there are reasons why we are waiting to build wealth our way. This chapter highlights a few of these roadblocks in the hopes that you can navigate your way beyond them to the legacy wealth you desire.

Roadblock 1: Legacy Wealth Is Business and Personal

Wealth is not self-perpetuating. It does not build, grow, and expand on its own. Wealth requires a vision, a strategy, consistent action, relationships, and defined outcomes for it to materialize into the value that matches the desires of the heart that is building it. It is for these reasons wealth manifests within a group process, a relationship with first your complete self (your history and legacy), then with your ability to create resources from the talents you possess (your pursuit, roadmap, and journey), then with your chosen community (macro; the business of you), and finally with your desired standard of living in this world (micro; the business of you). The tighter, more connected the relationships the fuller the life, the more realized the purpose, the deeper the faith, and the greater the value of the wealth.

Creating wealth is simple, but it is not easy. Along the road to wealth creation are blind spots that lead to rocky paths that stem from missed and skipped steps that are necessary to mitigate risks everyone encounters when pursuing the desires of their hearts. Risks are real; fear of them are distractions from what you desire most in life, to fully realize all you are with all you have. Sometimes fear keeps us safe, sometimes it holds us back; understanding your relationship with risk is knowing the difference.

The need to mitigate risk is how the road to wealth is narrowed by your choices in the midst of a wide array of options. This is your life journey after all, and to get what you want you must understand how to best protect and grow what you have. This is accomplished when you clarify your vision of what wealth will enable you to do in your everyday life. The level of risk you are willing to take is up to you, the level of wealth you will build is up to your choices about how to manage the risks along your NarrowRoad to legacy wealth.

Wealth requires you to attach to desired outcomes located further down the road, beyond what is readily seen. What is it that you really desire for your life, your family, your community? What is your role in bringing about these outcomes? Where must others assist? A large part of legacy wealth is the convergence of your faith and your finances; you have to believe in your ability to create wealth for yourself, however you define it. And that belief invites others to join you. Agreement can mitigate risks. Agreement requires communication with others about your desires and the fears that are attached to pursuing them. The further you go down the road, the more you will find yourself charting a path along a narrower road that is often less traveled. Until now custom navigation tools such as your NRID had yet to be created. For too long wealth was something hidden in the field of affluence and the upwardly mobile. But everyone in his or her own way wants to get there. Now is the time for you to stretch your ability to believe. We all can get out of the financial wilderness. This book has given you the steps, so why are you waiting?

Roadblock 2: The Way You Begin Is not the Way You End

The journey toward wealth is in its genesis an individual pursuit with a series of glimpses created excessively for your personal development, The first glimpse is one exclusively given to you through the lens of your legacy (Quadrant 1). The second glimpse is what begins your learning journey, unlocking your genius code to pursue opportunities unique to you (Quadrant 2), the third glimpse is what creates your mission with the talents you currently have in your possession to earn the income to build the seeds of your wealth (Quadrant 3). The fourth glimpse begins the collective movement forward through the exchange of your strengths for assistance with the navigating the roadmap to the desires of your heart and (Quadrant 4, Part 4).

Your pursuit of wealth as you define it is your business, and that business engages and exchanges with collective processes such as education, community, voting, crowd-funding, and equity investing. Staying focused on your pursuit by leveraging your personal systems for success while remaining aware of the necessary collective processes is how you navigate further down the road.

Everyone has a genesis and an exodus in their lives. Your genesis is the starting point of your journey. Your introduction to business began with your childhood —the family business. How your family managed the household operations and your role in it is the genesis of your life pursuit. So how did your family manage money? Which best describes your experience within this phase of development? What do you want to do differently? Where have you shifted your perspective to make those changes? What questions do you still have to increase your level of confidence in making these desired changes and mitigate risk? What must you do now to take that next step? What can't you do alone? Who must you ask for help? To build upon your genesis and get beyond the wilderness onto your NarrowRoad these are the questions you must answer for yourself. Your answers to these questions have been explored throughout this book, should you desire a wealth group to assist you in answering them and holding you accountable extend your journey along the NarrowRoad to www.mynarrowroad.com/wealthgroup.

By now you know the NarrowRoad journey through the wilderness leads to a custom-designed path toward legacy wealth. It is customized because it is based on your own choices and definition of wealth. It is meant to be stress-free, exciting, and filled with learning opportunities. Getting through the wilderness is owning your choices with your NarrowRoad identity you do this by ordering your steps to get to where you most desire to go. With your NRID you now have this tool to build your own system for success

Your Wealth Journey Is Dimensional

What may not be extremely clear is that the NarrowRoad has dimensions. Dimensions are aspects, inflection points. Each dimension further clarifies how you define wealth and what you desire it to be in your life.

To remove the obstacles blocking your legacy wealth perspective, look first at what you can afford to model differently for your family legacy, then explore how to best face whatever challenges appear before you, and move on. This is your contribution to legacy of your family business. It matters that you that you succeed in a pursuing what you see as most important to continue the legacy forward to wealth defined by you. Align yourself with your legacy perspective and you are on your way.

To pursue your dream of financial independence, organize (your power) people and money; prioritize what is important. Your partnership is with the priorities in your life and getting you and them beyond the financial wilderness.

To get out of the storm of doing all things on our own and at once, act on your mission—operate your business as a talent multiplier both intrapreneurially and entrepreneurially.

To build the life you want, speak your truth about wealth with those you trust and want to get there with you. Your share of the wealth enterprise involves a group.

To ensure you stay on your NarrowRoad, connect with a goal you consider important to reach. How far can you afford to look down the road now?

So Where Are You in the Wilderness?

You own your position in the wilderness with the answer to the following question: Why I have not gone beyond my present financial situation? Is a lack of order, a lack of structure? A lack of faith? Or not facing my financial truth?

For wealth to be real, you must believe it is possible for you on your terms, with your unique variables that create your wealth equation. Your wealth equation is how you define wealth on your terms. Lack of definition leads to lack of direction, which leads you along the crowded wide-open gate people find themselves facing when wandering in the financial wilderness with good intentions.

Wealth requires more than good intentions. It demands that you pay attention—to your vision, your thoughts, your actions, your speech. Wealth expects you to have desired outcomes. It is promised that once aligned you will be given the desires of your heart, but you must define what they are and how others can help you get there.

Ten years ago I knew I wanted wealth to be something less complicated. I marveled at how those with the audacious goals and determination did not always succeed at first, but something kept them moving forward. They seemed to attract success by the way they desired it. I recently attended my twentieth reunion at Hampton University, my beloved home by the sea. I had not been back since my tenth reunion. My father loved to go every year; it reminded him of the journey I had taken and how far I had come from a little girl hoping to become a woman pursuing dreams well-worn from both success and failure. As I walked the campus, remembering where my great-grandmother came to visit me sophomore year, where my father loved to sit by the water, close to where my mother enjoyed walking by the sailboats, I also began to realize Hampton represents the legacy wealth promise. One of the few historically Black colleges who has had the same president for generations, Hampton represents a vision that took time to mold, fund, support, and expand. I was able to see what was not so readily apparent twenty-four years ago when I began my contribution to the Hampton legacy. While the seeds were planted with me, it took twenty additional graduating classes to reveal it in its entirety. Many things I cherished about my Hampton experience are gone, but what remains are the memories as I share it in my narrative, the relationships I cherish with those who experienced what I experienced, and the ability to continue to play a role in the expansion of the vision for another twenty years.

Working in the financial-services industries in many roles with various responsibilities and perspectives, I have seen evolution of legacy to wealth. Where there were laws, rules, and regulations that kept segments of our population from owning and building wealth, things are changing. The Joint Center for Housing at Harvard reported that by 2025 there will be seventeen million new homeowners, and 76 percent of these new homeowners will be from diverse markets. Home ownership, a major driver of wealth creation, will become a standard in communities who three generations ago struggled with financing. The wheel continues to turn and so must we with it.

Along the NarrowRoad you will find the patterns within these four roles (vision, thought, action, speech) reveal your legacy, your strategy, your mission, and your purpose. Traveling the NarrowRoad will reveal your fears and deepest desires of your heart. When you take the ordered steps to connect the dots of these simple elements, you will trust and believe in the promise that wealth is possible for you. Legacy wealth is self-perpetuating. Legacy wealth connects the dots from the past to the present to the future. It creates a three-corded strand that is not easily broken once connected and tied to a future that often you have to "believe to eventually see." This is how your faith and finance connect to build from the wealth hidden within you.

The NarrowRoad meets you where you are in the wealth-creation process and helps you to chart a path to however far down the road you desire to go (legacy and its transfer). Hope is not the only thing that springs eternal. Wealth can spring forth eternal opportunities if you take the time to write the vision and make it plain so that generation after generation can run with it. Legacy wealth in this light is a system that ensures visions come to pass in their appointed time. No need to commit your life to a hustle when you have taken the time to write your legacy wealth blueprint that can pass on beyond you.

We are the best teachers but the worst students of our own lesson plans—walk your talk and live up to your standard. Things take time. Everything has a process. As my grandmother would often say, "The only thing God is not making any more of is time and land, so steward them appropriately."

Lessons Learned on the NarrowRoad

Reviewing Why We Are Waiting to Build Legacy Wealth

The glimpse in chapter 15 is that things take time. Everything has a process. The only thing God is not making any more of is time and land, so we must learn to steward resources unique to our lives and legacies appropriately. Legacy wealth is waiting for us to explore and develop it. Believe this and the wait is over.

If you wish to continue on the NarrowRoad, join the journey by visiting mynarrowroad.com and chart your path to legacy wealth today.

The following are questions to help you better understand the NarrowRoad you're traveling. Answer as honestly as you can (if you're honest with yourself, your road will narrow to a path conducive to your success). There are no right or wrong answers, even if they don't match everything you've read in this book—remember, for legacy wealth to be attainable, it must be defined by you and the choices you understand.

Why Are You Waiting?

Legacy is more than money. Remember the roles you play in your life as you answer these questions. Remember, your pursuit can teach future generations.

During your childhood, how did your family handle money?

____

____

____

What do you want to do differently?

____

____

____

What is your current financial situation?

____

____

____

What did you need to improve your financial situation?

____

____

____

____

What are you afraid of that can't you do alone?

___

___

___

What questions must you ask to get the help you need?

___

___

___

Invitation to Join NarrowRoad

As a reader of the book you are officially on the NarrowRoad™

Membership has privileges. The NarrowRoad™ is expanding its territory in cities across the country. Preparing men, women, pastors, businesses, and young professionals to build legacy wealth through crowd equity funding and other collective strategies. To be alerted of the activities and initiatives that will be spreading to communities near you please join the NarrowRoad™ journey.

Let's together not leave this world the way we found it.

Register your NRID by texting "NarrowRoad" to 610-200-6118.

Alternatively go to mynarrowroad.com/book

Appendix

What Is an accredited investor? Usually they are sophisticated investors who are financially savvy. In the United States, an accredited investor is someone who meets the requirements established by the Securities and Exchange Commission to participate in large-scale investment transactions. Individuals who are accredited investors meet at least one of the following criteria:

- ☐ Earn an annual individual income of more than $200,000 or a joint annual income of $300,000 for the last two years and have the reasonable expectation of maintaining the same level of income for the current year.

- ☐ Have a net worth exceeding $1 million, either individually or jointly with his or her spouse.

- ☐ Serve as a general partner, executive officer, director, or similar role for the issuer of a security being offered.

For more information, please visit the Securities and Exchange Commission site.

What Is a Non-Accredited Investor? A non-accredited investor is simply an investor who does not meet the Securities and Exchange Commission requirements to become an accredited investor.

Proposed Rules: Consistent with the JOBS Act, the proposed rules would among other things permit individuals to invest subject to certain thresholds, limit the amount of money a company can raise, require companies to disclose certain information about their offers, and create a regulatory framework for the intermediaries that would facilitate the crowd-funding transactions.

Under the proposed rules:

- ☑ A company would be able to raise a maximum aggregate amount of $1 million through crowd-funding offerings in a twelve-month period.
- ☑ Investors, over the course of a twelve-month period, would be permitted to invest up to:
- ☑ Two thousand dollars, or 5 percent of their annual income or net worth, whichever is greater, if both their annual income and net worth are less than $100,000.
- ☑ Ten percent of their annual income or net worth, whichever is greater, if either their annual income or net worth is equal to or more than $100,000. During the twelve-month period, these investors would not be able to purchase more than $100,000 of securities through crowd-funding.

http://www.sec.gov/News/PressRelease/Detail/PressRelease/1370540017677#.U_oXel7tKII.

Thank You's

Eleven years is a long time to work towards and focus on one thing. Along the road as it narrowed there were countless people who helped me in ways they may not even know. Not only do I thank you, I have and will continue to pray for you and your legacy wealth journey. I know that one day our paths will cross again and I will return the favor you bestowed on my life just when I needed it most. I am living proof that if you want to go far you must go together.

In the midst of the many (and I do mean many) who supported my journey as I narrowed my road there are a few who I must mention:

The Investors — those visionaries who planted financial seed into the journey and confirmed my path was for me: Bessie Pearl Horne (my grandmother), Sylvia Jolly (my mother), Vincent Jolly Sr. (my father, may he rest in peace), Vincent Jolly Jr.(my brother), Eulena B. Horne (my aunt), Avis Scott Schwartz (my cousin), Ophelia Foote (My great aunt), Jasmine Bellamy, Nichol Bradford, Miriam Torres, Tonia Spence, Dr. Marisa Rogers, Eston Griffin, Drs. Brenda and James Rogers, Arthur Roland, Asantewaa Phoenix, Tina Eskridge, Vaughn Fauria, Linwood and Kathi Jolly, Rev. William (Billy) Jolly (my cousin), Bill Jolly (my cousin), Mark Randall, Wilmont Allen, Joyce Ntim, & Bishop Leon J. Petty (rest in peace)

The Strategists — those thinkers whose expertise helped me gain confidence in believing in and building the NarrowRoad™: Stanley Tucker, Bennie L. Horne Jr. (my uncle), Charles Harris, Marcus Adams, Robert Barrimond, Carla Harris, Kathia and Shane Dennis, Dr. Cheryl Miller, Kizzie Bozeman, Glen Boykin, Barthaniel Werts, Michael Rapelyea, Christopher Nazzereth, Mark Randall, Joy Jordan, Lesley Steward, Rod Stanley, Dr. Peter Paris, Dr. Charles Adams, Dr. Shawn Copeland, Jacob Cobb Mays III, Nigel Henry, Terrence Damon Barclift, Trevor Ott, Che Brown, & Charles Wooding

The Builders —Those doers whose engagements with Torch Enterprises allowed me to perfect the NarrowRoad™ curricula and workshop materials - My Pastor clients, The fast girls, Alpha Phi Alpha Fraternity, Inc., Alpha Kappa Alpha Sorority, Inc., NAREB, UNCF, 1st District AME, Enon Tabernacle Baptist Church, Mocha Mom's, RIISE, Tabernacle International Deliverance Church Empowerment Network, countless entrepreneurs and their communities

The Connectors — those speakers who helped me build the NarrowRoad™ system by opening their mouths and spreading the word of my desire to elevate the standard of legacy to wealth in our communities: Rev. Charisse Tucker, Dr. George Fraser, Georgette Dixon, Cheryl McDonald, Brenda Wright, Greg Young, Marva Allen, Cerita Battle, Beverly Ferguson, C. Renee

Wilson, Mandala Jones, Doris Canty-Brown, Anika Khan, Pastor Rossie Francis, Carlos and Winifred Bell, Lorisa Bates, Tonia Petty, Renee Carracter, Janice Hopkins, Keisha Chandler, Michele Lawrence, Laura Roane, William D. Lyle, Edgar Carter

The Deliverers of Outcomes: Those chance moments that gave me the encouragement to keep on going at the bends in the road of this journey: 100 Black Men National Conferences, Wells Fargo legacy Wealth Events, Mocha Mom's National Conference, UNCF Legacy Wealth Breakfasts, NAACP Leadership Summit, Urban League National Conference, Thurgood Marshal Foundation Youth Conference, Bethune Cookman University's Woman's Conference, Wharton African American Alumni Network, NAREB SHIBA Events, NAREB National Conferences, George Fraser's PowerNetworking Conferences

Wide is the gate, narrow is the road, few find it and even fewer take it **until now**....

Lets build legacy wealth together.

I am looking forward to the jolly-good things that await us further down the road. The Promise thou it may seem to tarry is for an appointed time for you.